AF454340

SELECTIONS FROM THE PROSE WRITINGS OF JOHN HENRY CARDINAL NEWMAN

FOR THE USE OF SCHOOLS - ANNOTATED

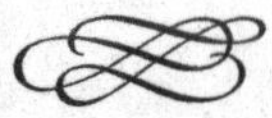

JOHN HENRY NEWMAN

ALICIA EDITIONS

CONTENTS

INTRODUCTION

It has come to be universally admitted that Cardinal Newman fulfills his own definition of a great author: "One whose aim is to give forth what he has within him; and from his very earnestness it happens that whatever be the splendor of his diction, or the harmony of his periods, he has with him the charm of an incommunicable simplicity.

"Whatever be his subject, high or low, he treats it suitably and for its own sake.... He writes passionately because he feels keenly; forcibly, because he conceives vividly; he sees too clearly to be vague; he is too serious to be otiose; he can analyze his subject, and therefore he is rich; he embraces it as a whole and in its parts, and therefore he is consistent; he has a firm hold of it, and therefore he is luminous.

"When his imagination wells up, it overflows in ornament; when his heart is touched, it thrills along his verse. He always has the right word for the right idea, and never a word too much....

"He expresses what all feel but cannot say; and his sayings pass into proverbs among his people, and his phrases become household words, idioms of their daily speech, which is tessellated with the rich fragments of his language, as we see in foreign lands the marbles of Roman grandeur worked into the walls and pavements of modern palaces."

Newman may be said to have handled England's prose as Shakespeare handled her verse. His language was wrought up little by little to a finish and refinement, a strength and a subtlety, thrown into the form of eloquence, beyond which no English writer of prose has gone. Nor is his excellence that of mere art in form; he possesses not only skill, which he calls an exercise of talent, but power—a second name for genius—which itself implies personality and points to inspiration.

His mind was large, logical, profoundly thoughtful, imaginative, intense, sincere, and above all, spiritual; his soul was keen, delicate, sympathetic, heroic; and his life, at once severe and tender, passionate and self-controlled, alone and unlonely, stands out in its loftiness and saintliness, a strange, majestic contrast to the agitation and turmoil of "confused passions, hesitating ideals, tentative virtues, and groping philanthropies" amidst which it was lived.

Both by word and work did Newman lead forth his generation on the long pilgrimage to the shrine of Truth, and England of the nineteenth century has no surer claim to holiness and genius for her great sons than that set upon John Henry Newman. He was born in London, 1801; studied, taught, and preached at Oxford; became the chief promoter of the Tractarian Movement of 1833; entered the Catholic Church in 1845; founded the Oratory at Birmingham, 1848; was created Cardinal by Pope Leo XIII. 1879; died at Edgbaston, 1890.

Any attempt to choose from the writings of Newman what seems most desirable for brief class studies is certain to be woefully embarrassed by the very wealth of matter; and apology for risking the choice would be due, were it not lost sight of in the desire to see a literary model so pure, varied, animated, forceful, luminous—"a thing of light and beauty"—given to our students.

What is more significant of the Life Book of the saintly Oxford Scholar than his self-written epitaph:

"Ex umbris et imaginibus in veritatem"?[1]

---

1. "Out of the shadows and phantasms and into the truth."

APPRECIATIONS

Newman's best essays display a delicate and flexible treatment of language, without emphasis, without oddity, which hardly arrests the attention at first,—the reader being absorbed in the argument or statement,—but which, in course of time, fascinates, as a thing miraculous in its limpid grace and suavity.

—Edmund Gosse's History of Modern English Literature.

The work of Newman reveals him as one of the great masters of graceful, scholarly, finished prose. It is individual, it has charm, and this is the secret of its power to interest. No writer of our time has reflected his mind and heart in his pages as has Newman. He has light for the intellect and warmth for the heart.

—A. J. George's Types of Literary Art.

Newman towers, with only three or four compeers, above his generation; and now that the benignity of his great nature has passed from our sight, its majesty is more evident year by year.

—Scudder's Modern English Poets.

The finish and urbanity of Newman's prose have been universally commended even by those who are most strenuously opposed to his opinions.

—H. J. Nicoll.

All the resources of a master of English style are at Newman's command: pure diction, clear arrangement, delicate irony, gracious dignity, a copious command of words combined with a chaste reserve in using them. All these qualities go to make up the charm of Newman's style—the finest flower that the earliest system of a purely classical education has produced.

—J. Jacobs's Literary Studies.

Newman combines a thoroughly classical training, a scholarly form, with the incommunicable and almost inexplicable power to move audiences and readers.

—George Saintsbury.

The pure style of Newman may be compared in its distinguishing quality to the atmosphere. It is at once simple and subtle, vigorous and elastic; it penetrates into every recess of its subject; it is transparent, allowing each object it touches to display its own proper color.

—H. E. Beeching's English Prose.

There are touching passages characteristic of Newman's writings which give them a peculiar charm. They are those which yield momentary glimpses of a very tender heart that has a burden of its own, unrevealed to man.... It is, as I have heard it described, as though he suddenly opened a book and gave you a glimpse for a moment of wonderful secrets, and then as quickly closed it.... In Newman's Sermons, how the old truth became new; how it came home, as he spoke, with a meaning never felt before! He laid his finger how gently, yet how powerfully, on some inner place in the hearer's heart, and told him things about himself he had never known till then. Subtlest truths, which it would have taken philosophers pages of circumlocution and big words to state, were dropped out by the way in a sentence or two of the most transparent Saxon. What delicacy of style, yet what strength! how simple, yet how suggestive! how penetrating, yet how refined! how homely, yet how tender-hearted! You might come away still not believing the tenets peculiar to the High Church System, but you would be harder than most men if you did not feel more than ever ashamed of coarseness, selfishness, worldliness, if you did not feel the things of faith brought closer to the soul.... Newman's innate and intense idealism is, perhaps, his most striking characteristic.... It is a thought of his, always deeply felt and many times repeated, that this visible world is but the outward shell of an invisible kingdom, a screen which hides from our view things far greater and more wonderful than any which we see, and that the unseen world is close to us and ever ready to break through the shell and manifest itself.

—Shairp.

Newman's great reputation for prose and the supreme interest attaching to his life seem to have obscured the fame he might have won as a poet. He was in poetry, as in theology, a more masculine Keble, but with all the real purity of Keble, with also the indispensable flavor of earth.

—H. Walker.

The *Dream of Gerontius* resembles Dante more than any other poetry written since the great Tuscan's time.

—Sir Henry Taylor.

The *Dream* is a rare poetic rendering into English verse of that high ritual which from the death-bed to the Mass of Supplication encompasses the faithful soul.... Newman has no marked affinities with English writers of his day. He is strikingly different from Macaulay, whose eloquence betrays the fury, as it is annealed in the fire, of the Western Celt. To Ruskin, who deliberately built up a monument, stately as the palace of Kubla Khan, he is a contrast, for the very reason that he does not handle words as if they were settings in architecture or colors in a palette; rather, he would look upon them as transparencies which let his meaning through. He is more like De Quincey, but again no player upon the organ for the sake of its music; and that which is common to both is the literary tradition of the eighteenth century enhanced by a power to which abstract and concrete yielded in almost equal degree.... With so prompt and intense an intellect at his call, there was no subject, outside purely technical criticism, which Newman could not have mastered.

—Barry's Literary Lives.

It is when Newman exerts his flexible and vivid imagination in depicting the deepest religious passion that we are most carried away by him and feel his great genius most truly.... Whether tried by the test of nobility, intensity, and steadfastness of his work, or by the test of the greatness of the powers which have been consecrated to that work, Cardinal Newman has been one of the greatest of our modern great men.

—R. H. Hutton's Life of Newman.

Newman's mind was world-wide. He was interested in everything that was going on in science, in the highest form of politics, in literature.... Nothing was too large for him, nothing too trivial, if it threw light upon the central question,—what man really is and what is his destiny.

—J. A. Froude.

In Newman's sketch of the influence of Abelard on his disciples is seen his belief in the immense power for good or ill of a dominating personality. And he himself supplied an object-lesson in his theory. Shairp, Froude, Church, Wilberforce, Gladstone, are only a few of those who have borne testimony to the personal magnetism which left its mark on the whole of thinking Oxford. "Cor ad cor loquitur," the motto chosen by Newman on his receiving the Cardinal's hat, expressed to him the whole reality of intercourse between man and man, and man and God.

—Wilfrid Ward's Problems and Persons.

Newman's mind swung through a wide arc, and thoughts apparently antagonistic often were to him supplemental each to each…. A
man of dauntless courage and profound thoughtfulness, while his
intellect was preëminently a logical one, both the heart and the moral
sense possessed with him their sacred tribunals in matters of reasoning
as well as of sentiment…. The extreme subtlety of his intelligence
opposed no hindrance to his power of exciting vehement emotion.

—*A. De Vere's Literary Reminiscences.*

PART I
CHARACTER SKETCHES

SAUL

"I gave them a king in mine anger, and took him away in my wrath."

— *HOSEA* XIII. 11.

The Israelites[1] seem to have asked for a king from an unthankful caprice and waywardness. The ill conduct, indeed, of Samuel's sons was the occasion of the sin, but "an evil heart of unbelief," to use Scripture language, was the real cause of it. They had ever been restless and dissatisfied, asking for flesh when they had manna[2], fretful for water, impatient of the wilderness, bent on returning to Egypt, fearing their enemies, murmuring against Moses[3]. They had miracles even to satiety; and then, for a change, they wished a king like the nations. This was the chief reason of their sinful demand. And further, they were dazzled with the pomp and splendor of the heathen monarchs around them, and they desired some one to fight their battles, some visible succor to depend on, instead of having to wait for an invisible Providence, which came in its own way and time, by little and little, being dispensed silently, or tardily, or (as they might consider) unsuitably. Their carnal hearts did not love the neighborhood of heaven; and, like the inhabitants of Gadara[4] afterwards, they prayed that Almighty God would depart from their coasts.

Such were some of the feelings under which they desired a king like the nations; and God at length granted their request. To punish them, He gave them a king *after their own heart*, Saul, the son of Kish, a Benjamite; of whom the text speaks in these terms, "I gave them a king in Mine anger, and took him away in My wrath."

There is, in true religion, a sameness, an absence of hue and brilliancy, in the eyes of the natural man; a plainness, austereness, and (what he considers) sadness. It is like the heavenly manna of which the Israelites complained, insipid, and at length wearisome, "like wafers made with honey." They complained that "their soul was dried away." "There is nothing at all," they said, "beside this manna, before our eyes.... We remember the fish, which we did eat in Egypt freely; the cucumbers, and the melons, and the leeks, and the onions, and the garlick."[5] Such were the dainty meats in which their soul delighted; and for the same reason they desired a king. Samuel had too much of primitive simplicity about him to please them, they felt they were behind the world, and clamored to be put on a level with the heathen.

Saul, the king whom God gave them, had much to recommend him to minds thus greedy of the dust of the earth. He was brave, daring, resolute; gifted, too, with strength of body as well as of mind—a circumstance which seems to have attracted their admiration. He is described in person as if one of those sons of Anak, before whose giant-forms the spies of the Israelites in the wilderness were as grasshoppers—"a choice young man, and a goodly; there was not amon the children of Israel a goodlier person than he: from his shoulders and upward he was higher than any of the people."[6] Both his virtues and his faults were such as became an eastern monarch, and were adapted to secure the fear and submission of his subjects. Pride, haughtiness, obstinacy, reserve, jealousy, caprice—these, in their way, were not unbecoming qualities in the king after whom their imaginations roved. On the other hand, the better parts of his character were of an excellence sufficient to engage the affection of Samuel himself.

As to Samuel, his conduct is far above human praise. Though injuriously treated by his countrymen, who cast him off after he had served them faithfully till he was "old and gray-headed,"[7] and who resolved on setting over themselves a king against his earnest entreaties, still we find no trace of coldness or jealousy in his behavior towards Saul. On his first meeting with him, he addressed him in the words of loyalty—"On whom is all the desire of Israel? is it not on thee, and on all thy father's house?" Afterwards, when he anointed him king, he "kissed him, and said, Is it not because the Lord hath anointed thee to be captain over His inheritance?" When he announced him to the people as their king, he said, "See ye him whom the Lord hath chosen, that there is none like him among all the people?" And, some time after, when Saul had irrecoverably lost God's favor, we are told, "Samuel came no more to see Saul until the day of his death: *nevertheless Samuel mourned for Saul*." In the next chapter he is even rebuked for immoderate grief—"How long wilt thou mourn for Saul, seeing I have rejected him from reigning over Israel?[8] Such sorrow speaks favorably for Saul as well as for Samuel; it is not only the grief of a loyal subject and a zealous prophet, but, moreover, of an attached friend; and, indeed, instances are recorded, in the first years of his reign, of forbearance, generosity, and neglect of self, which sufficiently account for the feelings with which Samuel regarded him. David[9], under very different circumstances, seems to have felt for him a similar affection.

The higher points of his character are brought out in instances such as the following: The first announcement of his elevation came upon him suddenly, but apparently without unsettling him. He kept it secret, leaving it to Samuel, who had made it to him, to publish it. "Saul said unto his uncle, He" (that is, Samuel) "told us plainly that the asses[10] were found. But of the matter of the kingdom, whereof Samuel spake *he told him not*." Nay, it would even seem he was averse to the dignity intended for him; for when the Divine lot fell upon him, he hid himself, and was not discovered by the people, without recourse to Divine assistance. The appointment was at first unpopular. "The children of Belial said, How shall this man save us? They despised him, and brought him no presents, *but he held his peace*." Soon the Ammonites[11] invaded the country beyond Jordan[12], with the avowed intention of subjugating it. The people sent to Saul for relief almost in despair; and the panic spread in the interior as well as among those whose country was immediately threatened. The history proceeds: "*Behold, Saul came after the herd out of the field*; and Saul said, What aileth the people that they weep? and they told him the tidings of the men of Jabesh. And the Spirit of God came upon Saul, and his anger was kindled greatly." His order for an immediate gathering throughout Israel was obeyed with the alacrity with which the multitude serve the strong-minded in times of danger. A decisive victory over the enemy followed; then the popular cry became, "Who is he that said, Shall Saul reign over us? bring the men, that we may put them to death. And Saul said, *There shall not a man be put to death this day*, for to-day the Lord hath wrought salvation in Israel."[13]

Thus personally qualified, Saul was, moreover, a prosperous king. He had been appointed t subdue the enemies of Israel, and success attended his arms. At the end of the fourteenth chapter, we read: "So Saul took the kingdom over Israel and fought against all his enemies on every side, against Moab, and against the children of Ammon, and against Edom, and against the kings of Zobah, and against the Philistines[14]; and whithersoever he turned himself, he vexed them. And he gathered an host, and smote the Amalekites, and delivered Israel out of the hands of them that spoiled them."

Such was Saul's character and success; his character faulty, yet not without promise; his success in arms as great as his carnal subjects could have desired. Yet, in spite of Samuel's private liking for him, and in spite of the good fortune which actually attended him, we find that from the beginning the prophet's voice is raised both against people and king in warnings and rebukes, which are omens of his destined destruction, according to the text, "I gave them a king in Mine anger, and took him away in My wrath." At the very time that Saul is publicly received as king, Samuel protests, "Ye have this day rejected your God, who Himself saved you out of all your adversities and your tribulations."[15] In a subsequent assembly of the people, in which he testified his uprightness, he says, "Is it not wheat harvest to-day? I will call unto the Lord, and He shall send thunder and rain; *that ye may perceive and see that your wickedness is great*, in asking you a king." Again, "If ye shall still do wickedly, ye shall be consumed, both ye and your king."[16] And after this, on the first instance of disobedience and at first sight no very heinous sin, the sentence of rejection is passed upon him: "Thy kingdom shall not continue; the Lord hath sought Him a man after His own heart."[17]

Here, then, a question may be raised——Why was Saul thus marked for vengeance from the beginning? Why these presages of misfortune, which from the first hung over him, gathered, fell in storm and tempest, and at length overwhelmed him? Is his character so essentially faulty that it must be thus distinguished for reprobation above all the anointed kings after him? Why, while David is called a man after God's own heart, should Saul be put aside as worthless?

This question leads us to a deeper inspection of, his character. Now, we know, the first duty of every man is the fear of God—a reverence for His word, a love of Him, and a desire to obey Him; and, besides, it was peculiarly incumbent on the king of Israel, as God's vicegerent[18], by virtue of his office, to promote His glory whom his subjects had rejected.

Now Saul "lacked this one thing." His character, indeed, is obscure, and we must be cautious while considering it; still, as Scripture is given us for our instruction, it is surely right to make the most of what we find there, and to form our judgment by such lights as we possess. It would appear, then, that Saul was never under the abiding influence of religion, or, in Scripture language, "the fear of God," however he might be at times moved and softened. Some men are inconsistent in their conduct, as Samson; or as Eli, in a different way; and yet may have lived by faith, though a weak faith. Others have sudden falls, as David had. Others are corrupted by prosperity, as Solomon[19]. But as to Saul, there is no proof that he had any deep-seated religious principle[20] at all; rather, it is to be feared, that his history is a lesson to us, that the "heart of unbelief" may exist in the very sight of God, may rule a man in spite of many natural advantages of character in the midst of much that is virtuous, amiable, and commendable.

Saul, it would seem, was naturally brave, active, generous, and patient; and what nature made him, such he remained, that is, without improvement; with virtues which had no value, because they required no effort, and implied the influence of no principle. On the other hand, when we look for evidence of his faith, that is, his practical sense of things unseen, we discover instead a deadness to all considerations not connected with the present world. It is his habit to treat prophet and priest with a coldness, to say the least, which seems to argue some great internal defect. It would not be inconsistent with the Scripture account of him, even should the real fact be, that (with some general notions concerning the being and providence of God) he doubted of the divinity of the Dispensation of which he was an instrument. The circumstance which first introduces him to the inspired history is not in his favor. While in search of his father's asses, which were lost, he came to the city where Samuel was; and though Samuel was now an old man, and from childhood known as the especial minister and prophet of the God of Israel, Saul seems to have considered him as a mere diviner, such as might be found among the heathen, who, for "the fourth part of a shekel[21] of silver," would tell him his way.

The narrative goes on to mention, that after his leaving Samuel "God gave him another heart," and on meeting a company of prophets, "the Spirit of God came upon him, and he prophesied among them." Upon this, "all that knew him beforetime" said, "What is this that is come unto the son of Kish: is Saul also among the prophets? ... therefore it became a proverb." From this narrative we gather, that his carelessness and coldness in religious matters were so notorious, that, in the eyes of his acquaintance, there was a certain strangeness and incongruity, which at once struck the mind, in his being associated with a school of the prophets.

Nor have we any reason to believe, from the after history, that the Divine gift, then first imparted, left any religious effect upon his mind. At a later period of his life we find him suddenly brought under the same sacred influence on his entering the school where Samuel taught; but, instead of softening him, its effect upon his outward conduct did but testify the fruitlessness of Divine grace when acting upon a will obstinately set upon evil.

The immediate occasion of his rejection was his failing under a specific trial of his obedience, as set before him at the very time he was anointed. He had collected with difficulty an army against the Philistines; while waiting for Samuel to offer the sacrifice, his people became dispirited, and began to fall off and return home. Here he was doubtless exposed to the temptation of taking unlawful measures to put a stop to their defection. But when we consider that the act to which he was persuaded was no less than that of his offering sacrifice[22]—he being neither priest nor prophet, nor having any commission thus to interfere with the Mosaic ritual—it is plain "his *forcing himself*" to do so (as he tenderly described his sin) was a direct profaneness—a profaneness which implied that he was careless about forms, which in this world will ever be essential to things supernatural, and thought it mattered little whether he acted in God's way or in his own.

After this, he seems to have separated himself from Samuel, whom he found unwilling to become his instrument, and to have had recourse to the priesthood instead. Ahijah or Ahimelech (as he is afterwards called), the high priest, followed his camp; and the ark, too, in spite of the warning conveyed by the disasters which attended the presumptuous use of it in the time of Eli. "And Saul said unto Ahijah, Bring hither the ark of God[23];" while it was brought, a tumult which was heard in the camp of the Philistines increased. On this interruption Saul irreverently put the ark aside, and went out to the battle. It will be observed, that there was no professed or intentional irreverence in Saul's conduct; he was still on the whole the same he had ever been. He outwardly respected the Mosaic ritual—about this time he built his first altar to the Lord,[24] and in a certain sense seemed to acknowledge God's authority. But nothing shows he considered that there was any vast distinction between Israel and the nations around them. He was *indifferent*, and cared for none of these things. The chosen people desired a king like the nations, and such a one they received.

After this he was commanded to "go and smite the sinners, the Amalekites, and utterly destroy them and their cattle." This was a judgment on them which God had long decreed, though He had delayed it; and He now made Saul the minister of His vengeance. But Saul performed it so far only as fell in with his own inclination and purposes. He smote, indeed, the Amalekites, and "destroyed all the people with the edge of the sword"—this exploit had its glory; the best of the flocks and herds he spared, and why? to sacrifice therewith to the Lord. But since God had expressly told him to destroy them, what was this but to imply, that Divine intimations had nothing to do with such matters? what was it but to consider that the established religion[25] was but a useful institution, or a splendid pageant suitable to the dignity of monarchy, but resting on no unseen supernatural sanction? Certainly he in no sense acted in the fear of God, with the wish to please Him, and the conviction that he was in His sight. One might consider it mere pride and willfulness in him, acting in his own way because it was his own (which doubtless it was in great measure), except that he appears to have had an eye to the feelings and opinions of men as to his conduct, though not to God's judgment. He "feared the people and obeyed their voice." Again, he spared Agag, the king of the Amalekites. Doubtless he considered Agag as "his brother," as Ahab afterwards called Ben-hadad. Agag was a king, and Saul observed towards him that courtesy and clemency which earthly monarchs observe one towards another, and rightly when no Divine command comes in the way. But the God of Israel required a king after His own heart, jealous of idolatry; the people had desired a king like the nations around them.

It is remarkable, moreover, that while he spared Agag, he attempted to exterminate the Gibeonites with the sword, who were tolerated in Israel by virtue of an oath taken in their favor by Joshua[26] and "the princes of the congregation." This he did "*in his zeal* to the children of Israel and Judah."[27]

From the time of his disobedience in the matter of Amalek, Samuel came no more to see Saul, whose season of probation was over. The evil spirit exerted a more visible influence upon him; and God sent Samuel to anoint David privately, as the future king of Israel. I need not trace further the course of moral degradation which is exemplified in Saul's subsequent history. Mere natural virtue wears away, when men neglect to deepen it into religious principle. Saul appears in his youth to be unassuming and forbearing; in advanced life he is not only proud and gloomy (as he ever was in a degree), but cruel, resentful, and hard-hearted, which he was not in his youth His injurious treatment of David is a long history; but his conduct to Ahimelech, the high priest, admits of being mentioned here. Ahimelech assisted David in his escape. Saul resolved on the death of Ahimelech and all his father's house.[28] On his guards refusing to execute his command, Doeg, a man of Edom, one of the nations which Saul was raised up to withstand, undertook the atrocious deed. On that day, eighty-five priests were slain. Afterwards Nob the city of the priests, was smitten with the edge of the sword, and all destroyed, "men and women, children and sucklings, and oxen, and asses, and sheep." That is, Saul executed more complete vengeance on the descendants of Levi, the sacred tribe, than on the sinners, the Amalekites, who laid wait for Israel in the way, on their going up from Egypt.

Last of all, he finishes his bad history by an open act of apostasy from the God of Israel. His last act is like his first, but more significant. He began, as we saw, by consulting Samuel as a diviner; this showed the direction of his mind. It steadily persevered in its evil way—and he ends by consulting a professed sorceress at Endor. The Philistines had assembled their hosts; Saul's heart trembled greatly—he had no advisers or comforters; Samuel was dead—the priests he had himself slain with the sword. He hoped, by magic rites, which he had formerly denounced, to foresee the issue of the approaching battle. God meets him even in the cave of Satanic delusions—but as an Antagonist. The reprobate king receives, by the mouth of dead Samuel, who had once anointed him, the news that he is to be "taken away in God's wrath"—that the Lord would deliver Israel, with him, into the hands of the Philistines, and that on the morrow he and his sons should be numbered with the dead.[29]

The next day "the battle went sore against him, the archers hit him; and he was sore wounded of the archers."[30] "Anguish came upon him,"[31] and he feared to fall into the hands of the uncircumcised[32]. He desired his armor-bearer to draw his sword and thrust him through therewith. On his refusing, he fell upon his own sword, and so came to his end.

---

1. **Introductory Note.** The sketches of Saul and David are contained in the third volume of *Parochial and Plain Sermons*. These discourses were delivered at Oxford before Newman's conversion to the Catholic Church. **Saul.** The first king of Israel reigned from 1091 to 1051 B.C. He ruled conjointly with Samuel the prophet eighteen years, and alone, twenty-two years. Samuel had been judge of Israel twelve years when the discontented Jews demanded a king, and Saul was elected by lot.
2. Miraculous food supplied to the Jews, wandering in the desert of Sin, after their exodus from Egypt. The taste of manna was that of flour mixed with honey.
3. Deliverer, lawgiver, ruler, and prophet of Israel, 1447 B.C. The author of the *Pentateuch* is probably the greatest figure of the Old Law and the most perfect type of Christ.
4. Noted for the miracle of casting out demons, wrought there by our Lord. The inhabitants in fear besought Him to leave their coasts. Mark v. 17.
5. Exod. xvi.; Numb. xi. 5
6. 1 Sam. ix. 2—*vide ibid.* x. 23
7. *Ibid.* xii. 2.
8. 1 Sam. ix. 20; x. 1, 24; xv. 35; xvi. 1.
9. The prophet and king famous as the royal psalmist. From his line sprang the Messias.
10. Saul, searching for his father's asses, was met by Samuel and anointed king.
11. Warlike heathen tribes probably descended from Lot. They dwelt near the Dead Sea; were very hostile to the Jews.
12. Largest river of Palestine, especially consecrated by the baptism of Christ in its waters; is called the river of judgment. An air line from the Sea of Galilee to the Dead Sea is sixty miles, but so tortuous is the Jordan, its length is two hundred miles.
13. 1 Sam. xi. 12, 13.

14. Gentiles beyond the Western Sea, frequently at war with the Hebrews. Samson, Saul, and David were famous for their victories over these powerful enemies.
15. 1 Sam. x. 19.
16. *Ibid.* xii. 17, 25.
17. *Ibid.* xiii. 14.
18. Representative as king. Before Saul the Jewish government was theocratic, *i.e.* directly from God.
19. Son and successor of David, called the wisest of men: built the temple; became exalted with pride; was punished for his sins: died probably unrepentant. A striking example of the vanity of human success unblessed by God.
20. A fundamental truth upon which conduct is consistently built. A conviction of the intellect and hence distinguished from instinct, disposition, feeling, often the spring of men's actions.
21. A silver coin worth about fifty-seven cents.
22. Sacrilegious in Saul, as the right was limited to the priesthood of Aaron.
23. A figure of the Christian Tabernacle; divinely ordained for the Mosaic worship; contained the covenant of God with His chosen people
24. 1 Sam. xiv. 35.
25. Inversion of Christ's command,—"Seek ye therefore first the kingdom of God and His justice and all these things shall be added unto you." Matthew vi.
26. Successor of Moses and leader of the Jews into the Promised Land.
27. Josh. ix. 2; 2 Sam. xxi. 1-5.
28. 1 Sam. xxii. 16.
29. 1 Sam. xxviii. 19.
30. *Ibid.* xxxi. 3.
31. 2 Sam. i. 9.
32. Term applied to all outside the Hebrew people. Circumcision, a figure of baptism, was the sign of covenant given by God to Abraham and his descendants.

EARLY YEARS OF DAVID

"Behold, I have seen a son of Jesse the Beth-lehemite, that is cunning in playing, and a mighty valiant man, and a man of war, and prudent in matters, and a comely person, and the Lord is with him."

— 1 SAMUEL XVI. 18.

Such is the account given to Saul of David, in many respects the most favored of the ancient Saints. David is to be accounted the most favored, first as being the principal type of Christ, next as being the author of great part of the book of Psalms[1], which have been used as the Church's form of devotion ever since his time. Besides, he was a chief instrument of God's providence, both in repressing idolatry and in preparing for the gospel; and he prophesied in an especial manner of that Saviour whom he prefigured and preceded. Moreover, he was the chosen king of Israel, a man after God's own heart, and blessed, not only in himself, but in his seed after him. And, further, to the history of his life a greater share is given of the inspired pages than to that of any other of God's favored servants. Lastly, he displays in his personal character that very temper of mind in which his nation, or rather human nature itself, is especially deficient. Pride and unbelief disgrace the history of the chosen people; the deliberate love of this world, which was the sin of Balaam[2], and the presumptuous willfulness which is exhibited in Saul. But David is conspicuous for an affectionate, a thankful, a loyal heart towards his God and defender, a zeal which was as fervent and as docile as Saul's was sullen, and as keen-sighted and as pure as Balaam's was selfish and double-minded. Such was the son of Jesse the Beth-lehemite; he stands midway between Abraham and his predicted seed, Judah[3] and the Shiloh[4], receiving and transmitting the promises; a figure of the Christ, and an inspired prophet, living in the Church even to the end of time, in his office, his history, and his sacred writings.

Some remarks on his early life, and on his character, as therein displayed, may profitably engage our attention at the present time.

When Saul was finally rejected for not destroying the Amalekites, Samuel was bid go to Bethlehem, and anoint, as future king of Israel, one of the sons of Jesse, who should be pointed out to him when he was come there. Samuel accordingly went thither and held a sacrifice; when, at his command, Jesse's seven sons were brought by their father, one by one, before the prophet; but none of them proved to be the choice of Almighty God. David was the youngest and out of the way, and it seemed to Jesse as unlikely that God's choice should fall upon him, as it appeared to Joseph's brethren and to his father, that he and his mother and brethren should, as his dreams foretold, bow down before him. On Samuel's inquiring, Jesse said, "There remaineth yet the youngest, and, behold, he keepeth the sheep." On Samuel's bidding, he was sent for. "Now he was ruddy," the sacred historian proceeds, "and withal of a beautiful countenance, and goodly to look to. And the Lord said, Arise, anoint him, for this is he." After Samuel had anointed him, "the Spirit of the Lord came upon David from that day forward." It is added, "But the Spirit of the Lord departed from Saul."

David's anointing[5] was followed by no other immediate mark of God's favor. He was tried by being sent back again, in spite of the promise, to the care of his sheep, till an unexpected occasion introduced him to Saul's court. The withdrawing of the Spirit of the Lord from Saul was followed by frequent attacks from an evil spirit, as a judgment upon him. His mind was depressed, and a "trouble," as it is called, came upon him, with symptoms very like those which we now refer to derangement. His servants thought that music, such, perhaps, as was used in the schools of the prophets, might soothe and restore him; and David was recommended by one of them for that purpose, in the words of the text: "Behold, I have seen a son of Jesse the Bethlehemite, that is cunning in playing, and a mighty valiant man, and a man of war, and prudent in matters, and a comely person, and the Lord is with him."

David came in the power of that sacred influence whom Saul had grieved and rejected. The Spirit which inspired his tongue guided his hand also, and his sacred songs[6] became a medicine to Saul's diseased mind. "When the evil spirit from God was upon Saul, ... David took an harp, and played with his hand; so Saul was refreshed, and was well, and the evil spirit departed from him." Thus he is first introduced to us in that character in which he still has praise in the Church, as "the anointed of the God of Jacob, and the sweet psalmist of Israel[7]

Saul "loved David greatly, and he became his armor-bearer;" but the first trial of his humility and patience was not over, while many other trials were in store. After a while he was a second time sent back to his sheep; and though there was war with the Philistines, and his three eldest brethren were in the army with Saul, and he had already essayed his strength in defending his father's flocks from wild beasts, and was "a mighty valiant man," yet he contentedly stayed at home as a private person, keeping his promise of greatness to himself, till his father bade him go to his brethren to take them a present from him, and report how they fared. An accident, as it appeared to the world, brought him forward. On his arrival at the army, he heard the challenge of the Philistine champion, Goliath of Gath[8]. I need not relate how he was divinely urged to engage the giant, how he killed him, and how he was, in consequence, again raised to Saul's favor; who, with an infirmity not inconsistent with the deranged state of his mind, seems to have altogether forgotten him.

From this time began David's public life; but not yet the fulfillment of the promise made to him by Samuel. He had a second and severer trial of patience to endure for many years; the trial of "being still" and doing nothing before God's time, though he had (apparently) the means in his hands of accomplishing the promise for himself. It was to this trial that Jeroboam afterwards showed himself unequal. He, too, was promised a kingdom, but he was tempted to seize upon it in his own way, and so forfeited God's protection.

David's victory over Goliath so endeared him to Saul, that he would not let him go back to his father's house. Jonathan, too, Saul's son, at once felt for him a warm affection, which deepened into a firm friendship. "Saul set him over the men of war, and he was accepted in the sight of all the people, and also in the sight of Saul's servants."[9] This prosperous fortune, however, did not long continue. As Saul passed through the cities from his victory over his enemies, the women of Israel came out to meet him, singing and dancing, and they said, "Saul hath slain his thousands, and David his ten thousands." Immediately the jealous king was "very wroth, and the saying displeased him"; his sullenness returned; he feared David as a rival; and "eyed him from that day and forward." On the morrow, as David was playing before him, as at other times, Saul threw his javelin at him. After this, Saul displaced him from his situation at his court, and sent him to the war, hoping so to rid himself of him by his falling in battle; but, by God's blessing, David returned victorious.

In a second war with the Philistines, David was successful as before; and Saul, overcome with gloomy and malevolent passions, again cast at him with his javelin, as he played before him, with the hope of killing him.

This repeated attempt on his life drove David from Saul's court; and for some years after, that is, till Saul's death, he was a wanderer upon the earth, persecuted in that country which was afterwards to be his own kingdom. Here, as in his victory over Goliath, Almighty God purposed to show us, that it was *His* hand which set David on the throne of Israel. David conquered his enemy by a sling and stone, in order, as he said at the time, that all ... might know "that the Lord saveth not with sword and spear; for the battle is the Lord's."[10] Now again, but in a different way, His guiding providence was displayed. As David slew Goliath without arms, so now he refrained himself and used them not, though he possessed them. Like Abraham, he traversed the land of promise "as a strange land,"[11] waiting for God's good time. Nay, far more exactly, even than to Abraham, was it given to David to act and suffer that life of faith which the Apostle[12] describes, and by which "the elders obtained a good report." By faith he wandered about, "being destitute, afflicted, evil-entreated, in deserts, and in mountains, and in dens, and in caves of the earth." On the other hand, through the same faith, he "subdued kingdoms, wrought righteousness, obtained promises, waxed valiant in fight, turned to flight the armies of the aliens." On escaping from Saul, he first went to Samuel to ask his advice. With him he dwelt some time. Driven thence by Saul he went to Bethlehem, his father's city, then to Ahimelech, the high priest, at Nob. Thence he fled, still through fear of Saul, to Achish, the Philistine king of Gath; and finding his life in danger there, he escaped to Adullam, where he was joined by his kindred, and put himself at the head of an irregular band of men, such as, in the unsettled state of the country, might be usefully and lawfully employed against the remnant of the heathen. After this he was driven to Hareth, to Keilah, which he rescued from the Philistines, to the wilderness of Ziph among the mountains, to the wilderness of Maon, to the strongholds of Engedi, to the wilderness of Paran. After a time he again betook himself to Achish, king of Gath, who gave him a city; and there it was that the news was brought him of the death of Saul in battle, which was the occasion of his elevation first to the throne of Judah, afterwards to that of all Israel, according to the promise of God made to him by Samuel.

It need not be denied that, during these years of wandering, we find in David's conduct instances of infirmity and inconsistency, and some things which, without being clearly wrong, are yet strange and startling in so favored a servant of God. With these we are not concerned, except so far as a lesson may be gained from them for ourselves. We are not at all concerned with them as regards our estimate of David's character. That character is ascertained and sealed by the plain word of Scripture, by the praise of Almighty God, and is no subject for our criticism; and if we find in it traits which we cannot fully reconcile with the approbation divinely given to him, we must take it in faith to be what it is said to be, and wait for the future revelations of Him who "overcomes when He is judged." Therefore I dismiss these matters now, when I am engaged in exhibiting the eminent obedience and manifold virtues of David. On the whole his situation during these years of trial was certainly that of a witness for Almighty God, one who does good and suffers for it, nay, suffers on rather than rid himself from suffering by any unlawful act.

Now, then, let us consider what was, as far as we can understand, his especial grace, what is his gift; as faith was Abraham's distinguishing virtue, meekness the excellence of Moses, self-mastery the gift especially conspicuous in Joseph[13].

This question may best be answered by considering the purpose for which he was raised up. When Saul was disobedient, Samuel said to him, "Thy kingdom shall not continue: the Lord hath sought Him *a man after His own heart*, and the Lord hath commanded him to be captain over His people, because thou hast not kept that which the Lord commanded thee."[14] The office to which first Saul and then David were called was different from that with which other favored men before them had been entrusted. From the time of Moses[15], when Israel became a nation, God had been the king of Israel, and His chosen servants, not delegates, but mere organs of His will. Moses did not direct the Israelites by his own wisdom, but he spake to them, as God spake from the pillar of the cloud. Joshua, again, was merely a sword in the hand of God. Samuel was but His minister and interpreter. God acted, the Israelites "stood still and saw" His miracles, then followed. But, when they had rejected Him from being king over them, then their chief ruler was no longer a mere organ of His power and will, but had a certain authority intrusted to him, more or less independent of super-natural direction; and acted, not so much *from* God, as *for* God, and *in the place of* God. David, when taken from the sheepfolds "to feed Jacob His people and Israel His inheritance," "fed them," in the words of the Psalm, "with a faithful and true heart; and ruled them prudently with all his power."[16] From this account of his office, it is obvious that his very first duty was that of *fidelity to Almighty God* in the trust committed to him. He had power put into his hands, in a sense in which neither Moses had it nor Samuel. He was charged with a certain office, which he was bound to administer according to his ability, so as best to promote the interests of Him who appointed him. Saul had neglected his Master's honor; but David, in this an eminent type of Christ, "came to do God's will" as a viceroy in Israel, and, as being tried and found faithful, he is especially called "a man after God's own heart."

David's peculiar excellence, then, is that of *fidelity to the trust committed to him*; a firm, uncompromising, single-hearted devotion to the cause of his God, and a burning zeal for His honor.

This characteristic virtue is especially illustrated in the early years of his life which have engaged our attention. He was tried therein and found faithful; before he was put in power, it was proved whether he could obey. Till he came to the throne, he was like Moses or Samuel, an instrument in God's hands, bid do what was told him and nothing more;—having borne this trial of obedience well, in which Saul had failed, then at length he was intrusted with a sort of discretionary power, to use in his Master's service.

Observe how David was tried, and what various high qualities of mind he displayed in the course of the trial. First, the promise of greatness was given him, and Samuel anointed him. Still he stayed in the sheepfolds; and though called away by Saul for a time, yet returned contentedly when Saul released him from attendance. How difficult is it for such as know they have gifts suitable to the Church's need to refrain themselves, till God make a way for their use! and the trial would be the more severe in David's case, in proportion to the ardor and energy of his mind; yet he fainted not under it. Afterwards for seven years, as the time appears to be, he withstood the strong temptation, eve before his eyes, of acting without God's guidance, when he had the means of doing so. Though skillful in arms, popular with his countrymen, successful against the enemy, the king's son-in-law[17], and on the other hand grievously injured by Saul, who not only continually sought his life, but even suggested to him a traitor's conduct by accusing him of treason, and whose life was several times in his hands, yet he kept his honor pure and unimpeachable. He feared Go and honored the king; and this at a time of life especially exposed to the temptations of ambition.

There is a resemblance between the early history of David and that of Joseph[18]. Both distinguished for piety in youth, the youngest and the despised of their respective brethren, they are raised, after a long trial to a high station, as ministers of God's Providence. Joseph was tempted to a degrading adultery; David was tempted by ambition. Both were tempted to be traitors to their masters and benefactors. Joseph's trial was brief; but his conduct under it evidenced settled habits of virtue which he could call to his aid at a moment's notice. A long imprisonment followed, the consequence of hi obedience, and borne with meekness and patience; but it was no part of his temptation, because, when once incurred, release was out of his power. David's trial, on the other hand, lasted for years, and grew stronger as time went on. His master, too, far from "putting all that he had into his hand,"[19] sought his life. Continual opportunity of avenging himself incited his passions; self-defense, and the Divine promise, were specious arguments to seduce his reason. Yet he mastered his heart—

he was "still"; he kept his hands clean and his lips guileless—he was loyal throughout—and in due time inherited the promise.

Let us call to mind some of the circumstances of his steadfastness recorded in the history.

He was about twenty-three years old when he slew the Philistine; yet, when placed over Saul's men of war, in the first transport of his victory, we are told he "behaved himself wisely."[20] When fortune turned, and Saul became jealous of him, still "David behaved himself wisely in all his ways, and the Lord was with him." How like is this to Joseph under different circumstances! "Wherefore when Saul saw that he behaved himself very wisely he was afraid of him; and all Israel and Judah loved David." Again, "And David behaved himself more wisely than all the servants of Saul, so that his name was much set by." Here, in shifting fortunes, is evidence of that staid, composed frame of mind in his youth, which he himself describes in the one hundred and thirty-first Psalm. "My heart is not haughty, nor mine eyes lofty.... Surely I have behaved and quieted myself, as a child that is weaned of his mother."

The same modest deportment marks his subsequent conduct. He consistently seeks counsel of God. When he fled from Saul he went to Samuel; afterwards we find him following the directions of the prophet Gad, and afterwards of Abiathar the high priest.[21] Here his character is in full contrast to the character of Saul. Further, consider his behavior towards Saul, when he had him in his power; it displays a most striking and admirable union of simple faith and unblemished loyalty.

Saul, while in pursuit of him, went into a cave in Engedi. David surprised him there, and his companions advised to seize him, if not to take his life. They said, "Behold the day of which the Lord said unto thee."[22] David, in order to show Saul how entirely his life had been in his power, arose and cut off a part of his robe privately. After he had done it, his "heart smote him" even for this slight freedom, as if it were a disrespect offered towards his king and father. "He said unto his men, The Lord forbid that I should do this thing unto my master, the Lord's anointed, to stretch forth mine hand against him, seeing he is the anointed of the Lord." When Saul left the cave, David followed him and cried, "My Lord the king. And when Saul looked behind him, David stooped with his face to the earth and bowed himself." He hoped that he could now convince Saul of his integrity. "Wherefore hearest thou men's words," he asked, "saying, Behold, David seeketh thy hurt? Behold, this day thine eyes have seen how that the Lord had delivered thee to-day into mine hand in the cave: and some bade me kill thee.... Moreover, my father, see, yea see the skirt of thy robe in my hand: for in that I cut off the skirt of thy robe, and killed thee not, know thou and see, that there is neither evil nor transgression in mine hand, and I have not sinned against thee: yet thou huntest my soul to take it. The Lord judge between me and thee, and the Lord avenge me of thee: but mine hand shall not be upon thee.... After whom is the king of Israel come out? after whom dost thou pursue? after a dead dog, after a flea. The Lord therefore judge ... and see, and plead my cause, and deliver me out of thine hand." Saul was for the time overcome; he said, "Is this thy voice, my son David? and Saul lifted up his voice and wept." And he said, "Thou art more righteous than I; for thou hast rewarded me good, whereas I have rewarded thee evil." He added, "And now, behold, I know well that thou shalt surely be king." At another time David surprised Saul in the midst of his camp, and his companion would have killed him; but he said, "Destroy him not, for who can stretch forth his hand against the Lord's anointed and be guiltless?"[23] Then, as he stood over him, he meditated sorrowfully on his master's future fortunes, while he himself refrained from interfering with God's purposes. "Surely the Lord shall smite him; or his day shall come to die; or he shall descend into battle and perish." David retired from the enemy's camp; and when at a safe distance, roused Saul's guards, and blamed them for their negligent watch, which had allowed a stranger to approach the person of their king. Saul was moved the second time; the miserable man, as if waking from a dream which hung about him, said, "I have sinned; return, my son David ... behold, I have played the fool, and have erred exceedingly." He added, truth overcoming him, "Blessed be thou, my son David; thou shalt both do great things, and also shalt still prevail." How beautiful are these passages in the history of the chosen king of Israel! How do they draw our hearts towards him, as one whom in his private character it must have been an extreme privilege and a great delight to know! Surely, the blessings of the patriarchs[24] descended in a united flood upon "the lion of the tribe of Judah," the type of the true Redeemer who was to come. He inherits the prompt faith and magnanimity of Abraham; he is simple as Isaac; he is humble as Jacob; he has

the youthful wisdom and self-possession, the tenderness, the affectionateness, and the firmness of Joseph. And, as his own especial gift, he
has an overflowing thankfulness, an ever-burning devotion, a zealous
fidelity to his God, a high unshaken loyalty towards his king, an heroic
bearing in all circumstances, such as the multitude of men see to be
great, but cannot understand. Be it our blessedness, unless the wish be
presumptuous, so to acquit ourselves in troubled times; cheerful amid
anxieties, collected in dangers, generous towards enemies, patient in
pain and sorrow, subdued in good fortune! How manifold are the
ways of the Spirit, how various the graces which He imparts; what
depth and width is there in that moral truth and virtue for which we
are created! Contrast one with another the Scripture Saints; how
different are they, yet how alike! how fitted for their respective circumstances, yet how unearthly, how settled and composed in the faith and
fear of God! As in the Services, so in the patterns of the Church, God
has met all our needs, all our frames of mind. "Is any afflicted? let him
pray; is any merry? let him sing Psalms."[25] Is any in joy or in sorrow?
there are Saints at hand to encourage and guide him. There is Abraham
for nobles, Job for men of wealth and merchandise, Moses for patriots,
Samuel for rulers, Elijah for reformers, Joseph for those who rise into
distinction; there is Daniel for the forlorn, Jeremiah for the persecuted,
Hannah for the downcast, Ruth for the friendless, the Shunamite for
the matron, Caleb for the soldier, Boaz for the farmer, Mephibosheth
for the subject; but none is vouchsafed to us in more varied lights, and
with more abundant and more affecting lessons, whether in his history
or in his writings, than he whose eulogy is contained in the words of
the text, as cunning in playing, and a mighty valiant man, and prudent
in matters, and comely in person, and favored by Almighty God. May
we be taught, as he was, to employ the gifts, in whatever measure
given us, to God's honor and glory, and to the extension of that true
and only faith which is the salvation of the soul!

---

1. One hundred and fifty inspired hymns of praise, joy, thanksgiving, and repentance,
   composed chiefly by David. Humanly speaking, they form the most exquisite lyric
   poetry extant, and in their strong, majestic beauty are most suitable to the Divine
   Offices of the Church.
2. An Oriental prophet of Mesopotamia, 1500 B.C. Sent for by the Moabite king to
   curse the Israelites.
3. The fourth son of Jacob and Leah.

4. The Messias.
5. To signify that the kingship, like the priesthood, is a sacred office, *all* power coming from God.
6. The inspired music of David was the means of restoring grace to the troubled spirit of Saul. Browning's *Saul* paints strikingly the character of the shepherd boy and of the distracted old king.
7. 2 Sam. xxiii. 1.
8. A type of the giant, Sin; also of Lucifer, overcome by the meek Christ, who is prefigured by David.
9. 1 Sam. xviii. 5.
10. 1 Sam. xvii. 47.
11. Heb. xi. 9.
12. St. Paul, who recounts to the Hebrews his sufferings for Christ.
13. Son of Jacob; governor of Egypt under Pharaoh.
14. 1 Sam. xiii. 14.
15. A fine distinction between the theocratic and the royal government of Israel.
16. Ps. lxxviii. 71-73.
17. Saul in envy married his daughter Michol to David "that she might prove a stumbling-block to him."
18. Note the consistent and forcible parallel.
19. Gen. xxxix. 4.
20. 1 Sam. xviii. 5-30.
21. *Ibid.* xxii. 5, 20; xxiii. 6.
22. 1 Sam. xxiv.4.
23. 1 Sam. xxvi. 9.
24. This passage illustrates the exquisite choice of words, the perfect finish of sentence, and the wonderful beauty of thought characteristic of Newman.
25. James v. 13.

BASIL AND GREGORY

"What are these discourses that you hold one with another, as you walk and are sad?"

1

I

The instruments raised up by Almighty God for the accomplishment of His purposes are of two kinds, equally gifted with faith and piety, but from natural temper and talent, education, or other circumstances, differing in the means by which they promote their sacred cause. The first of these are men of acute and ready mind, with accurate knowledge of human nature, and large plans, and persuasive and attractive bearing, genial, sociable, and popular, endued with prudence, patience, instinctive tact and decision in conducting matters, as well as boldness and zeal. Such in a measure we may imagine the single-minded, the intrepid, the much-enduring Hildebrand[2], who, at a time when society was forming itself anew, was the Saviour, humanly speaking, of the City of God[3]. Such, in an earlier age, was the majestic Ambrose[4]; such the never-wearied Athanasius. These last-named luminaries of the Church came into public life early, and thus learned how to cope with the various tempers, views, and measures of the men they encountered there. Athanasius was but twenty-seven when he went with Alexander to the Nicene Council, and the year after he was Bishop of Alexandria. Ambrose was consecrated soon after the age of thirty.

Again, there is an instrument in the hand of Providence, of less elaborate and splendid workmanship, less rich in its political endowments, so to call them, yet not less beautiful in its texture, nor less precious in its material. Such is the retired and thoughtful student, who remains years and years in the solitude of a college or a monastery, chastening his soul in secret, raising it to high thought and single-minded purpose, and when at length called into active life, conducting himself with firmness, guilelessness, zeal like a flaming fire, and all the sweetness of purity and integrity. Such an one is often unsuccessful in his own day; he is too artless to persuade, too severe to please; unskilled in the weaknesses of human nature, unfurnished in the resources of ready wit, negligent of men's applause, unsuspicious, open-hearted, he does his work, and so leaves it; and it seems to die; but in the generation after him it lives again, and on the long run it is difficult to say which of the two classes of men has served the cause of truth the more effectually. Such, perhaps, was Basil, who issued from the solitudes of Pontus[5] to rule like a king, and minister like the lowest in the kingdom; yet to meet little but disappointment, and to quit life prematurely in pain and sorrow. Such was his friend, the accomplished Gregory, however different in other respects from him, who left his father's roof for an heretical city, raised a church there, and was driven back into retirement by his own people, as soon as his triumph over the false creed was secured. Such, perhaps, St. Peter Damiani in the middle age; such St. Anselm, such St. Edmund. No comparison is, of course, attempted here between the religious excellence of the two descriptions of men; each of them serves God according to the peculiar gifts given to him. If we might continue our instances by way of comparison, we should say that St. Paul reminds us of the former, and Jeremiah of the latter...

It often happens that men of very dissimilar talents and tastes are attracted together by their very dissimilitude. They live in intimacy for a time, perhaps a long time, till their circumstances alter, or some sudden event comes, to try them. Then the peculiarities of their respective minds are brought out into action; and quarrels ensue, which end in coolness or separation. It would not be right or true to say that this is exemplified in the instance of the two blessed Apostles, whose "sharp contention[6]" is related in the Book of Acts; for they had been united in spirit once for all by a Divine gift; and yet their strife reminds us of what takes place in life continually. And it so far resembled the everyday quarrels of friends, in that it arose from difference of temper and character in those favored servants of God. The zealous heart of the Apostle of the Gentiles endured not the presence of one who had swerved in his course; the indulgent spirit of Barnabas felt that a first fault ought not to be a last trial. Such are the two main characters which are found in the Church,—high energy, and sweetness of temper; far from incompatible, of course, united in Apostles, though in different relative proportions, yet only partially combined in ordinary Christians, and often altogether parted from each other.

This contrast of character, leading, first, to intimacy, then to differences, is interestingly displayed, though painfully, in one passage of the history of Basil and Gregory: Gregory the affectionate, the tender-hearted, the man of quick feelings, the accomplished, the eloquent preacher,—and Basil, the man of firm resolve and hard deeds, the high-minded ruler of Christ's flock, the diligent laborer in the field of ecclesiastical politics. Thus they differed; yet not as if they had not much in common still; both had the blessing and the discomfort of a sensitive mind; both were devoted to an ascetic life; both were men of classical tastes; both were special champions of the Catholic creed; both were skilled in argument, and successful in their use of it; both were in highest place in the Church, the one Exarch of Cæsarea, the other Patriarch of Constantinople. I will now attempt to sketch the history of their intimacy.

II

Basil and Gregory were both natives of Cappadocia, but here, again, under different circumstances; Basil was born of a good family, and with Christian ancestors: Gregory was the son of the Bishop of Nazianzus, who had been brought up an idolater, or rather an Hypsistarian, a mongrel sort of religionist, part Jew, part Pagan. He was brought over to Christianity by the efforts of his wife Nonna, and at Nazianzus admitted by baptism into the Church. In process of time he was made bishop of that city; but not having a very firm hold of the faith, he was betrayed in 360 into signing the Ariminian creed[7], which caused him much trouble, and from which at length his son recovered him. Cæsarea being at no unsurmountable distance from Nazianzus, the two friends had known each other in their own country; but their intimacy began at Athens, whither they separately repaired for the purposes of education. This was about A.D. 350, when each of them was twenty-one years of age. Gregory came to the seat of learning shortly before Basil, and thus was able to be his host and guide on his arrival; but fame had reported Basil's merits before he came, and he seems to have made his way, in a place of all others most difficult to a stranger, with a facility peculiar to himself. He soon found himself admired and respected by his fellow-students; but Gregory was his only friend, and shared with him the reputation of talents and attainments. They remained at Athens four or five years; and, at the end of the time, made the acquaintance of Julian, since of evil name in history as the Apostate. Gregory thus describes in after life his early intimacy with Basil:

> *"Athens and letters followed on my stage;*
> *Others may tell how I encountered them;—*
> *How in the fear of God, and foremost found*
> *Of those who knew a more than mortal lore;—*
> *And how, amid the venture and the rush*
> *Of maddened youth with youth in rivalry,*
> *My tranquil course ran like some fabled spring,*
> *Which bubbles fresh beneath the turbid brine;*
> *Not drawn away by those who lure to ill,*
> *But drawing dear ones to the better part.*
> *There, too, I gained a further gift of God,*
> *Who made me friends with one of wisdom high,*
> *Without compeer in learning and in life.*
> *Ask ye his name?—in sooth, 'twas Basil, since*
> *My life's great gain,—and then my fellow dear*
> *In home, and studious search, and knowledge earned.*
> *May I not boast how in our day we moved*
> *A truest pair, not without name in Greece;*
> *Had all things common, and one only soul*

The friends had been educated for rhetoricians, and their oratorical powers were such, that they seemed to have every prize in prospect which a secular ambition could desire. Their names were known far and wide, their attainments acknowledged by enemies, and they themselves personally popular in their circle of acquaintance. It was under these circumstances that they took the extraordinary resolution of quitting the world together,—extraordinary the world calls it, utterly perplexed to find that any conceivable objects can, by any sane person, be accounted better than its own gifts and favors. They resolved to seek baptism of the Church, and to consecrate their gifts to the service of the Giver. With characters of mind very different—the one grave, the other lively; the one desponding, the other sanguine; the one with deep feelings, the other with feelings acute and warm;—they agreed together in holding, that the things that are seen are not to be compared to the things that are not seen. They quitted the world, while it entreated them to stay.

What passed when they were about to leave Athens represents as in a figure the parting which they and the world took of each other. When the day of valediction arrived, their companions and equals, nay, some of their tutors, came about them, and resisted their departure by entreaties, arguments, and even by violence. This occasion showed, also, their respective dispositions; for the firm Basil persevered, and went; the tender-hearted Gregory was softened, and stayed awhile longer. Basil, indeed, in spite of the reputation which attended him, had, from the first, felt disappointment with the celebrated abode of philosophy and literature; and seems to have given up the world from a simple conviction of its emptiness.

"He," says Gregory, "according to the way of human nature, when, on suddenly falling in with what we hoped to be greater, we find it less

than its fame, experienced some such feeling, began to be sad, grew
impatient, and could not congratulate himself on his place of residence.
He sought an object which hope had drawn for him; and he called
Athens 'hollow blessedness.'"

Gregory himself, on the contrary, looked at things more cheerfully;
as the succeeding sentences show.

"Thus Basil; but I removed the greater part of his sorrow, meeting it
with reason, and smoothing it with reflections, and saying (what was
most true) that character is not at once understood, nor except by long
time and perfect intimacy; nor are studies estimated, by those who are
submitted to them, on a brief trial and by slight evidence. Thus I reas-
sured him, and by continual trials of each other, I bound myself to
him."

— ORAT. 43.

III

Yet Gregory had inducements of his own to leave the world, not to
insist on his love of Basil's company. His mother had devoted him to
God, both before and after his birth; and when he was a child he had a
remarkable dream, which made a great impression upon him.

"While I was asleep," he says in one of his poems, which runs thus in
prose, "a dream came to me, which drew me readily to the desire of
chastity. Two virgin forms, in white garments, seemed to shine close to
me. Both were fair and of one age, and their ornament lay in their want
of ornament, which is a woman's beauty. No gold adorned their neck,
nor jacinth; nor had they the delicate spinning of the silkworm. Their
fair robe was bound with a girdle, and it reached down to their ankles.
Their head and face were concealed by a veil, and their eyes were fixed
on the ground. The fair glow of modesty was on both of them, as far as
could be seen under their thick covering. Their lips were closed in
silence, as the rose in its dewy leaves. When I saw them, I rejoiced
much; for I said that they were far more than mortals. And they in turn
kept kissing me, while I drew light from their lips, fondling me as a

41

dear son. And when I asked who and whence the women were, the one
answered, 'Purity,' the other, 'Sobriety'; 'We stand by Christ, the King,
and delight in the beauty of the celestial virgins. Come, then, child,
unite thy mind to our mind, thy light to our light; so shall we carry thee
aloft in all brightness through the air, and place thee by the radiance of
the immortal Trinity.'"

— CARM. P. 930.

He goes on to say, that he never lost the impression this made upon
him, as "a spark of heavenly fire," or "a taste of divine milk and honey."

As far, then, as these descriptions go, one might say that Gregory's
abandonment of the world arose from an early passion, as it may be
called, for a purity higher than his own nature; and Basil's, from a
profound sense of the world's nothingness and the world's defile-
ments. Both seem to have viewed it as a sort of penitential exercise, as
well as a means towards perfection.

When they had once resolved to devote themselves to the service of
religion, the question arose, how they might best improve and employ
the talents committed to them. Somehow, the idea of marrying and
taking orders, or taking orders and marrying, building or improving
their parsonages, and showing forth the charities, the humanities, and
the gentilities of a family man, did not suggest itself to their minds.
They fancied that they must give up wife, children, property, if they
would be perfect; and, this being taken for granted, that their choice
lay between two modes of life, both of which they regarded as
extremes. Here, then, for a time, they were in some perplexity. Gregory
speaks of two ascetic disciplines, that of the solitary or hermit, and that
of the secular; one of which, he says, profits a man's self, the other his
neighbor. Midway, however, between these lay the Cœnobite, or what
we commonly call the monastic; removed from the world, yet acting in
a certain select circle. And this was the rule which the friends at length
determined to adopt, withdrawing from mixed society in order to be of
the greater service to it. .The following is the passage in which Gregory
describes the life which was the common choice of both of them:

> *"Fierce was the whirlwind of my storm-toss'd mind,*
> *Searching,'mid holiest ways, a holier still.*

Long had I nerved me, in the depths to sink
Thoughts of the flesh, and then more strenuously.
Yet, while I gazed upon diviner aims,
I had not wit to single out the best:
For, as is aye the wont in things of earth,
Each had its evil, each its nobleness.
I was the pilgrim of a toilsome course,
Who had o'erpast the waves, and now look'd round,
With anxious eye, to track his road by land.
Then did the awful Thesbite's[8] image rise,
His highest Carmel[9], and his food uncouth;
The Baptist wealthy in his solitude;
And the unencumbered sons of Jonadab.
But soon I felt the love of holy books,
The spirit beaming bright in learned lore,
Which deserts could not hear, nor silence tell.
Long was the inward strife, till ended thus:—
I saw, when men lived in the fretful world,
They vantaged other men, but risked the while
The calmness and the pureness of their hearts.
They who retired held an uprighter port,
And raised their eyes with quiet strength towards heaven;
Yet served self only, unfraternally.
And so, 'twixt these and those, I struck my path,
To meditate with the free solitary,
Yet to live secular, and serve mankind."

---

1. **Introductory Note.** These Essays on the Fathers are to be found in *Historical Sketches*, Vol. III. They were written to illustrate the tone and mode of thought, the habits and manners of the early times of the Church. **Athens.** Most of those who sought Attic wisdom were natures without control. "Basil and Gregory were spoiled for subtle, beautiful, luxurious Athens. They walked their straight and loving road to God, with the simplicity which alone could issue out of the intense purpose of their lives —the love and service of Christ their Lord."
2. St. Gregory VII, one of the greatest among the great Roman pontiffs. He combated the evils of the eleventh century, within and without the Church, and effected incalculable good, especially in the war of Investitures waged against Henry IV of Germany.
3. The Church.
4. Archbishop of Milan, noted for zeal in spreading the faith; remembered for his fearlessrebuke of the Emperor Theodosius.

5. Part of Cappadocia in Asia Minor; founded by Alexander the Great.
6. See Acts of the Apostles xv. 39.
7. Similar to that of the Greek Church.
8. Elias, who dwelt on Carmel, as did St. John the Baptist, in most rigorous penance.
9. A mountain on the coast of Palestine, noted in sacred history.

AUGUSTINE AND THE VANDALS

"The just perisheth, and no man layeth it to heart; and men of mercy
are taken away, for there is none to understand; for the just man is
taken away from before the face of evil."

I

I began by directing the reader's attention to the labors of two
great bishops, who restored the faith of Christianity where it
had long been obscured. Now, I will put before him, by way of
contrast, a scene of the overthrow of religion,—the extinction of a
candlestick,—effected, too, by champions of the same heretical creed[1]
which Basil and Gregory successfully resisted. It will be found in the
history of the last days of the great Augustine, Bishop of Hippo, in
Africa. The truth triumphed in the East by the power of preaching; it
was extirpated in the South by the edge of the sword.

Though it may not be given us to appropriate the prophecies of the
Apocalypse[2] to the real events to which they belong, yet it is impossible to read its inspired pages, and then to turn to the dissolution of
the Roman empire, without seeing a remarkable agreement, on the
whole, between the calamities of that period and the sacred prediction.
There is a plain announcement in the inspired page, of "Woe, woe,

woe, to the inhabitants of the earth"; an announcement of "hail and fire mingled with blood," the conflagration of "trees and green grass," the destruction of ships, the darkening of the sun, and the poisoning of the rivers over a third of their course. There is a clear prophecy of revolutions on the face of the earth and in the structure of society. And, on the other hand, let us observe how fully such general foretokenings are borne out, among other passages of history, in the Vandalic[3] conquest of Africa.

The coast of Africa, between the great desert and the Mediterranean, was one of the most fruitful and opulent portions of the Roman world. The eastern extremity of it was more especially connected with the empire, containing in it Carthage, Hippo, and other towns, celebrated as being sees of the Christian Church, as well as places of civil importance. In the spring of the year 428, the Vandals, Arians by creed, and barbarians by birth and disposition, crossed the Straits of Gibraltar, and proceeded along this fertile district, bringing with them devastation and captivity on every side. They abandoned themselves to the most savage cruelties and excesses. They pillaged, ravaged, burned, massacred all that came in their way, sparing not even the fruit trees, which might have afforded some poor food to the remnant of the population, who had escaped from them into caves, the recesses of the mountains, or into vaults. Twice did this desolating pestilence sweep over the face of the country.

The fury of the Vandals was especially exercised towards the memorials of religion. Churches, cemeteries, monasteries, were objects of their fiercest hatred and most violent assaults. They broke into the places of worship, cut to pieces all internal decorations, and then set fire to them. They tortured bishops and clergy with the hope of obtaining treasure. The names of some of the victims of their ferocity are preserved. Mansuetus, Bishop of Utica, was burnt alive; Papinianus, Bishop of Vite, was laid upon red-hot plates of iron. This was near upon the time when the third General Council was assembling at Ephesus, which, from the insecure state of the roads, and the universal misery which reigned among them, the African bishops were prevented from attending. The Clergy, the religious brotherhoods, the holy virgins, were scattered all over the country. The daily sacrifice was stopped, the sacraments could not be obtained, the festivals of the Church passed unnoticed. At length, only three cities remained unvisited by the general desolation,—Carthage, Hippo, and Cirtha.

II

Hippo was the see of St. Austin, then seventy-four years of age (forty almost of which had been passed in ministerial labors), and warned, by the law of nature, of the approach of dissolution. It was as if the light of prosperity and peace were fading away from the African Church, as sank the bodily powers of its great earthly ornament and stay. At this time, when the terrors of the barbaric invasion spread on all sides, a bishop wrote to him to ask whether it was allowable for the ruler of a Church to leave the scene of his pastoral duties in order to save his life. Different opinions had heretofore been expressed on this question. In Augustine's own country Tertullian had maintained that flight was unlawful, but he was a Montanist[4] when he so wrote. On the other hand, Cyprian had actually fled, and had defended his conduct when questioned by the clergy of Rome. His contemporaries, Dionysius of Alexandria, and Gregory of Neocæsarea, had fled also; as had Polycarp before them, and Athanasius after them.

Athanasius also had to defend his flight, and he defended it, in a work still extant, thus: First, he observes, it has the sanction of numerous Scripture precedents. Thus, in the instance of confessors under the old covenant, Jacob fled from Esau, Moses from Pharao, David from Saul; Elias concealed himself from Achab three years, and the sons of the prophets were hid by Abdias in a cave from Jezebel. In like manner under the Gospel, the disciples hid themselves for fear of the Jews, and St. Paul was let down in a basket over the wall at Damascus. On the other hand, no instance can be adduced of overboldness and headstrong daring in the saints of Scripture. But our Lord Himself is the chief exemplar of fleeing from persecution. As a child in arms He had to flee into Egypt. When He returned, He still shunned Judea, and retired to Nazareth. After raising Lazarus, on the Jews seeking His life, "He walked no more openly among them," but retreated to the neighborhood of the desert. When they took up stones to cast at Him, He hid Himself; when they attempted to cast Him down headlong, He made His way through them; when He heard of the Baptist's death, He retired across the lake into a desert place, apart. If it be said that He did so, because His time was not yet come, and that when it was come, He delivered up Himself, we must ask, in reply, how a man can know that his time is come, so as to have a right to act as Christ acted? And since we do not know, we must have patience; and, till God by His own act determines the time, we must "wander in sheepskins and goatskins," rather than take the matter into our own hands; as even Saul, the persecutor, was left by David in the hands of God, whether He would "strike him, or his day should come to die, or he should go down to battle and perish."

If God's servants, proceeds Athanasius, have at any time presented themselves before their persecutors, it was at God's command: thus Elias showed himself to Achab; so did the prophet[5] from Juda, to Jeroboam[6]; and St. Paul appealed to Cæsar. Flight, so far from implying cowardice, requires often greater courage than not to flee. It is a greater trial of heart. Death is an end of all trouble; he who flees is ever expecting death, and dies daily. Job's life was not to be touched by Satan, yet was not his fortitude shown in what he suffered? Exile is full of miseries. The after-conduct of the saints showed they had not fled for fear. Jacob, on his death-bed, contemned death, and blessed each of the twelve Patriarchs; Moses returned, and presented himself before Pharao; David was a valiant warrior; Elias rebuked Achab and Ochazias; Peter and Paul, who had once hid themselves, offered themselves to martyrdom at Rome. And so acceptable was the previous flight of these men to Almighty God, that we read of His showing them some special favor during it. Then it was that Jacob had the vision of Angels; Moses saw the burning bush; David wrote his prophetic Psalms; Elias raised the dead, and gathered the people on Mount Carmel. How would the Gospel ever have been preached throughout the world, if the Apostles had not fled? And, since their time, those, too, who have become martyrs, at first fled; or, if they advanced to meet their persecutors, it was by some secret suggestion of the Divine Spirit. But, above all, while these instances abundantly illustrate the rule of duty in persecution, and the temper of mind necessary in those who observe it, we have that duty itself declared in a plain precept by no other than our Lord: "When they shall persecute you in this city," He says, "flee into another;" and "let them that are in Judea flee unto the mountains."

Thus argues the great Athanasius, living in spirit with the saints departed, while full of labor and care here on earth. For the arguments on the other side, let us turn to a writer, not less vigorous in mind, but less subdued in temper. Thus writes Tertullian on the same subject, then a Montanist, a century and a half earlier: Nothing happens, he says, without God's will. Persecution is sent by Him, to put His servants to the test; to divide between good and bad: it is a trial; what man has any right to interfere? He who gives the prize, alone can assign the combat. Persecution is more than permitted, it is actually appointed by Almighty God. It does the Church much good, as leading Christians to increased seriousness while it lasts. It comes and goes at God's ordering. Satan could not touch Job, except so far as God gave permission. He could not touch the Apostles, except as far as an opening was allowed in the words, "Satan hath desired to have you, but I have prayed for thee," Peter, "and thou, being once converted, confirm thy brethren." We pray, "Lead us not into temptation, but deliver us from evil;" why, if we may deliver ourselves? Satan is permitted access to us, either for punishment, as in Saul's case, or for our chastisement. Since the persecution comes from God, we may not lawfully avoid it, nor can we avoid it. We cannot, because He is all powerful; we must not, because He is all good. We should leave the matter entirely to God. As to the command of fleeing from city to city, this was temporary. It was intended to secure the preaching of the Gospel to the nations. While the Apostles preached to the Jews,—till they had preached to the Gentiles,—they were to flee; but one might as well argue, that we now are not to go "into the way of the Gentiles," but to confine ourselves to "the lost sheep of the house of Israel," as that we are now to "flee from city to city." Nor, indeed, was going from city to city a flight; it was a continued preaching; not an accident, but a rule: whether persecuted or not, they were to go about; and before they had gone through the cities of Israel, the Lord was to come. The command contemplated only those very cities. If St. Paul escaped out of "Damascus by night, yet afterwards, against the prayers of the disciples and the prophecy of Agabus, he went up to Jerusalem. Thus the command to flee did not last even through the lifetime of the Apostles; and, indeed, why should God introduce persecution, if He bids us retire from it? This is imputing inconsistency to His acts. If we want texts to justify our not fleeing, He says, "Whoso shall confess Me before men, I will confess him before My Father." "Blessed are they that suffer persecution;" "He that shall persevere to the end, he shall be saved;" "Be not afraid of them that kill the body;" "Whosoever does not carry his cross and come after Me, cannot be My disciple." How are these texts fulfilled when a man flees. Christ, who is our pattern, did not more than pray, "If it be possible, let this chalice pass:" we, too, should both stay and pray as He did. And it is expressly told us, that "We also ought to lay down our lives for the brethren." Again, it is said, "Perfect charity casteth out fear;" he who flees, fears; he who fears, "is not perfected in charity." The Greek proverb is sometimes urged, "He who flees, will fight another day;" yes, and he may flee another day, also. Again, if bishops, priests, and deacons flee, why must the laity stay? or must they flee also? "The good shepherd," on the contrary, "layeth down his life for his sheep"; whereas, the bad shepherd "seeth the wolf coming, and leaveth the sheep, and fleeth." At no time, as Jeremiah, Ezekiel, and Zechariah tell us, is the flock in greater danger of being scattered than when it loses its shepherd. Tertullian ends thus: "This doctrine, my brother, perhaps appears to you hard; nay, intolerable. But recollect that God has said, 'He that can take, let him take it;' that is, he who receives it not, let him depart. He who fears to suffer cannot belong to Him who has suffered. He who does not fear to suffer is perfect in love, that is, of God. Many are called, few are chosen. Not he who would walk the broad way is sought out by God, but he who walks the narrow." Thus the ingenious and vehement Tertullian.

III

With these remarks for and against flight in persecution, we shall be prepared to listen to Augustine on the subject; I have said, it was brought under his notice by a brother bishop, with reference to the impending visitation of the barbarians. His answer happily is preserved to us, and extracts from it shall now be set before the reader.

"To his Holy Brothers and Fellow-bishop Honoratus, Augustine sends Health in the Lord

"I thought the copy of my letter to our brother Quodvultdeus, which I sent to you, would have been sufficient, dear brother, without the task you put on me of counseling you on the proper course to pursue under our existing dangers. It was certainly a short letter; yet I included every question which it was necessary to ask and answer, when I said that no persons were hindered from retiring to such fortified places as they were able and desirous to secure; while, on the other hand, we might not break the bonds of our ministry, by which the love of Christ has engaged us not to desert the Church, where we are bound to serve. The following is what I laid down in the letter I refer to: 'It remains, then,' I say, 'that, though God's people in the place where we are be ever so few, yet, if it does stay, we, whose ministration is necessary to its staying, must say to the Lord, Thou art our strong rock and place of defense.' "But you tell me that this view is not sufficient for you, from an apprehension lest we should be running counter to our Lord's command and example, to flee from city to city. Yet is it conceivable that He meant that our flocks, whom He bought with His own blood, should be deprived of that necessary ministration without which they cannot live? Is He a precedent for this, who was carried in flight into Egypt by His parents when but a child, before He had formed Churches which we can talk of His leaving? Or, when St. Paul was let down in a basket through a window, lest the enemy should seize him, and so escaped his hands, was the Church of that place bereft of its necessary ministration, seeing there were other brethren stationed there to fulfill what was necessary? Evidently it was their wish that he, who was the direct object of the persecutors' search, should preserve himself for the sake of the Church. Let then, the servants of Christ, the ministers of His word and sacraments, do in such cases as He enjoined or permitted. Let such of them, by all means, flee from city to city, as are special objects of persecution; so that they who are not thus attacked desert not the Church, but give meat to those their fellow-servants, who they know cannot live without it. But in a case when all classes—I mean bishops, clergy, and people—are in some common danger, let not those who need the aid of others be deserted by those whom they need. Either let one and all remove into some fortified place, or, if any are obliged to remain, let them not be abandoned by those who have to supply their ecclesiastical necessity, so that they may survive in common, or suffer in common what their Father decrees they should undergo."

Then he makes mention of the argument[7] of a certain bishop, that "if our Lord has enjoined upon us flight, in persecutions which may ripen into martyrdom, much more is it necessary to flee from barren sufferings in a barbarian and hostile invasion," and he says, "this is true and reasonable, in the case of such as have no ecclesiastical office to tie them"; but he continues:

"Why should men make no question about obeying the precept of fleeing from city to city, and yet have no dread of 'the hireling who seeth the wolf coming, and fleeth, because he careth not for the sheep'? Why do they not try to reconcile (as they assuredly can) these two incontrovertible declarations of our Lord, one of which suffers and commands flight, the other arraigns and condemns it? And what other mode is there of reconciling them than that which I have above laid down? viz., that we, the ministers of Christ, who are under the pressure of persecution, are *then* at liberty to leave our posts, when no flock is left for us to serve; or again, when, though there be a flock, yet there are others to supply our necessary ministry, who have not the same reason for fleeing,—as in the case of St. Paul; or, again, of the holy Athanasius, bishop of Alexandria, who was especially sought after by the emperor Constantius, while the Catholic people, who remained together in Alexandria, were in no measure deserted by the other ministers. But when the people remain, and the ministers flee, and the ministration is suspended, what is that but the guilty flight of hirelings, who care not for the sheep? For then the wolf will come,—not man, but the devil, who is accustomed to persuade such believers to apostasy, who are bereft of the daily ministration of the Lord's Body; and by your, not knowledge, but ignorance of duty, the weak brother will perish, for whom Christ died.

"Let us only consider, when matters come to an extremity of danger, and there is no longer any means of escape, how persons flock together to the Church, of both sexes, and all ages, begging for baptism, or reconciliation, or even for works of penance, and one and all of them for consolation, and the consecration and application of the sacraments. Now, if ministers are wanting, what ruin awaits those, who depart from this life unregenerate or unabsolved! Consider the grief of their believing relatives, who will not have them as partakers with themselves in the rest of eternal life; consider the anguish of the whole multitude, nay, the cursings of some of them, at the absence of ministration and ministers. "It may be said, however, that the ministers of

God ought to avoid such imminent perils, in order to preserve themselves for the profit of the Church for more tranquil times. I grant it where others are present to supply the ecclesiastical ministry, as in the case of Athanasius. How necessary it was to the Church, how beneficial, that such a man should remain in the flesh, the Catholic faith bears witness, which was maintained against the Arians by his voice and his love. But when there is a common danger, and when there is rather reason to apprehend lest a man should be thought to flee, not from purpose of prudence, but from dread of dying, and when the example of flight does more harm than the service of living does good, it is by no means to be done. To be brief, holy David withdrew himself from the hazard of war, lest perchance he should 'quench the light of Israel,' at the instance of his people, not on his own motion. Otherwise, he would have occasioned many imitators of an inactivity which they had in that case ascribed, not to regard for the welfare of others, but to cowardice."

Then he goes on to a further question, what is to be done in a case where all ministers are likely to perish, unless some of them take to flight? or when persecution is set on foot only with the view of reaching the ministers of the Church? This leads him to exclaim:

"O, that there may be then a quarrel between God's ministers, *who* are to remain, and *who* to flee, lest the Church should be deserted, whether by all fleeing or all dying! Surely there will ever be such a quarrel, where each party burns in its own charity, yet indulges the charity of the other. In such a difficulty, the lot seems the fairest decision, in default of others. God judges better than man in perplexities of this sort; whether it be His will to reward the holier among them with the crown of martyrdom, and to spare the weak, or again, to strengthen the latter to endure evil, removing those from life whom the Church of God can spare the better. Should it, however, seem inexpedient to cast lots,—a measure for which I cannot bring precedent,—at least, let no one's flight be the cause of the Church's losing those ministrations which, in such dangers, are so necessary and so imperative. Let no one make himself an exception, on the plea of having some particular grace, which gives him a claim to life, and therefore to flight.

"It is sometimes supposed that bishops and clergy, remaining at their posts in dangers of this kind, mislead their flocks into staying, by their example. But it is easy for us to remove this objection or imputation, by frankly telling them not to be misled by our remaining. 'We are remaining for your sake,' we must say, 'lest you should fail to obtain such ministration, as we know to be necessary to your salvation in Christ. Make your escape, and you will then set us free.' The occasion for saying this is when there seems some real advantage in retiring to a safer position. Should all or some make answer, 'We are in His hands from whose anger no one can flee anywhere; whose mercy every one may find everywhere, though he stir not, whether some necessary tie detains him, or the uncertainty of safe escape deters him'; most undoubtedly such persons are not to be left destitute of Christian ministrations. "I have written these lines, dearest brother, in truth, as I think, and in sure charity, by way of reply, since you have consulted me; but not as dictating, if, perchance, you may find some better view to guide you. However, better we cannot do in these perils than pray the Lord our God to have mercy upon us."

— EP. 228.

IV

The luminous judgment, the calm faith, and the single-minded devotion which this letter exhibits, were fully maintained in the conduct of the far-famed writer, in the events which followed. It was written on the first entrance of the Vandals into Africa, about two years before they laid siege to Hippo; and during this interval of dreadful suspense and excitement, as well as of actual suffering, amid the desolation of the Church around him, with the prospect of his own personal trials, we find this unwearied teacher carrying on his works of love by pen, and word of mouth,—eagerly, as knowing his time was short, but tranquilly, as if it were a season of prosperity...

His life had been for many years one of great anxiety and discomfort, the life of one dissatisfied with himself, and despairing of finding the truth. Men of ordinary minds are not so circumstanced as to feel the misery of irreligion[8]. That misery consists in the perverted and discordant action of the various faculties and functions of the soul, which have lost their legitimate governing power, and are unable to regain it, except at the hands of their Maker. Now the run of irreligious men do not suffer in any great degree from this disorder, and are not miserable; they have neither great talents nor strong passions; they have not within them the materials of rebellion in such measure as to threaten their peace. They follow their own wishes, they yield to the bent of the moment, they act on inclination, not on principle, but their motive powers are neither strong nor various enough to be trouble-some. Their minds are in no sense under rule; but anarchy is not in their case a state of confusion, but of deadness; not unlike the internal condition as it is reported of eastern cities and provinces at present, in which, though the government is weak or null, the body politic goes on without any great embarrassment or collision of its members one with another, by the force of inveterate habit. It is very different when the moral and intellectual principles are vigorous, active, and devel-oped. Then, if the governing power be feeble, all the subordinates are in the position of rebels in arms; and what the state of a mind is under such circumstances, the analogy of a civil community will suggest to us. Then we have before us the melancholy spectacle of high aspira-tions without an aim, a hunger of the soul unsatisfied, and a never ending restlessness and inward warfare of its various faculties. Gifted minds, if not submitted to the rightful authority of religion, become the most unhappy and the most mischievous. They need both an object to feed upon, and the power of self-mastery; and the love of their Maker, and nothing but it, supplies both the one and the other. We have seen in our own day, in the case of a popular poet, an impressive instance of a great genius throwing off the fear of God, seeking for happiness in the creature, roaming unsatisfied from one object to another, breaking his soul upon itself, and bitterly confessing and imparting his wretchedness to all around him. I have no wish at all to compare him to St. Augustine; indeed, if we may say it without presumption, the very different termination of their trial seems to indicate some great difference in their respective modes of encountering it. The one dies of premature decay, to all appearance, a hardened infidel; and if he is still to have a name, will live in the mouths of men by writings at once blasphemous and immoral: the other is a Saint and Doctor of the Church. Each makes confessions, the one to the saints, the other to the powers of evil. And does not the difference of the two discover itself in some measure, even to our eyes, in the very history of their wanderings and pinings? At least, there is no appearance in St. Augustine's case of that dreadful haughtiness, sullenness, love of singularity, vanity, irritability, and misanthropy, which were too certainly the characteristics of our own countryman. Augustine was, as his early history shows, a man of affectionate and tender feelings, and open and amiable temper; and, above all, he sought for some excellence external to his own mind, instead of concentrating all his contemplations on himself. But let us consider what his misery was; it was that of a mind imprisoned, solitary, and wild with spiritual thirst; and forced to betake itself to the strongest excitements, by way of relieving itself of the rush and violence of feelings, of which the knowledge of the Divine Perfections was the true and sole sustenance. He ran into excess, not from love of it, but from this fierce fever of mind. "I sought what I might love,"[9] he says in his Confessions, "in love with loving, and safety I hated, and a way without snares. For within me was a famine of that inward food, Thyself, my God; yet throughout that famine I was not hungered, but was without any longing for incorruptible sustenance, not because filled therewith, but the more empty, the more I loathed it. For this cause my soul was sickly and full of sores; it miserably cast itself forth, desiring to be scraped by the touch of objects of sense."—iii. I.

"O foolish man that I then was," he says elsewhere, "enduring impatiently the lot of man! So I fretted, sighed, wept, was distracted; had neither rest nor counsel. For I bore about a shattered and bleeding soul, impatient of being borne by me, yet where to repose it I found not; not in calm groves, nor in games and music, nor in fragrant spots, nor in curious banquetings, nor in indulgence of the bed and the couch, nor, finally, in books or poetry found it repose. All things looked ghastly, yea, the very light. In groaning and tears alone found I a little refreshment. But when my soul was withdrawn from them, a huge load of misery weighed me down. To Thee, O Lord, it ought to have been raised, for Thee to lighten; I knew it, but neither could, nor would; the more, since when I thought of Thee, Thou wast not to me any solid or substantial thing. For Thou wert not Thyself, but a mere phantom, and my error was my God. If I offered to discharge my load thereon, that it might rest, it glided through the void, and came rushing down against me; and I had remained to myself a hapless spot, where I could neither

be, nor be from thence. For whither should my heart flee from my
heart? whither should I flee from myself? whither not follow myself?
And yet I fled out of my country; for so should mine eyes look less for
him, where they were not wont to see him."

— IV. 12.

He is speaking in this last sentence of a friend he had lost, whose
death-bed was very remarkable, and whose dear familiar name he
apparently has not courage to mention. "He had grown from a child
with me," he says, "and we had been both schoolfellows and playfel-
lows." Augustine had misled him into the heresy which he had
adopted himself, and when he grew to have more and more sympathy
in Augustine's pursuits, the latter united himself to him in a closer intimacy. Scarcely had he thus given him his heart, when God took him.

"Thou tookest him," he says, "out of this life, when he had scarce
completed one whole year of my friendship, sweet to me above all
sweetness in that life of mine. A long while, sore sick of a fever, he lay
senseless in the dews of death, and being given over, he was baptized
unwitting; I, meanwhile little regarding, or presuming that his soul
would retain rather what it had received of me than what was wrought
on his unconscious body."

The Manichees, it should be observed, rejected baptism. He
proceeds:

"But it proved far otherwise; for he was refreshed and restored. Forthwith, as soon as I could speak with him (and I could as soon as he was
able, for I never left him, and we hung but too much upon each other),
I essayed to jest with him, as though he would jest with me at that
baptism, which he had received, when utterly absent in mind and feeling, but had now understood that he had received. But he shrunk from
me, as from an enemy; and with a wonderful and sudden freedom
bade me, if I would continue his friend, forbear such language to him.
I, all astonished and amazed, suppressed all my emotions till he should
grow well, and his health were strong enough for me to deal with him
as I would. But he was taken away from my madness, that with Thee

57

he might be preserved for my comfort: a few days after, in my absence,
he was attacked again by fever, and so departed."

— IV. 8.

V

From distress of mind Augustine left his native place, Thagaste, and came to Carthage, where he became a teacher in rhetoric. Here he fell in with Faustus, an eminent Manichean bishop and disputant, in whom, however, he was disappointed; and the disappointment abated his attachment to his sect, and disposed him to look for truth elsewhere. Disgusted with the license which prevailed among the students at Carthage, he determined to proceed to Rome, and disregarding and eluding the entreaties of his mother, Monica[10], who dreaded his removal from his own country, he went thither. At Rome he resumed his professions; but inconveniences as great, though of another kind, encountered him in that city; and upon the people of Milan sending for a rhetoric reader, he made application for the appointment, and obtained it. To Milan then he came, the city of St. Ambrose, in the year of our Lord 385.

Ambrose, though weak in voice, had the reputation of eloquence; and Augustine, who seems to have gone with introductions to him, and was won by his kindness of manner, attended his sermons with curiosity and interest. "I listened," he says, "not in the frame of mind which became me, but in order to see whether his eloquence answered, what was reported of it: I hung on his words attentively, but of the matter I was but an unconcerned and contemptuous hearer."—v. 23. His impression of his style of preaching is worth noticing: "I was delighted with the sweetness of his discourse, more full of knowledge, yet in manner less pleasurable and soothing, than that of Faustus." Augustine was insensibly moved: he determined on leaving the Manichees, and returning to the state of a catechumen in the Catholic Church, into which he had been admitted by his parents. He began to eye and muse upon the great bishop of Milan more and more, and tried in vain to penetrate his secret heart, and to ascertain the thoughts and feelings which swayed him. He felt he did not understand him. If the respect and intimacy of the great could make a man happy, these advantages he perceived Ambrose to possess; yet he was not satisfied that he was a happy man. His celibacy seemed a drawback: what constituted his hidden life? or was he cold at heart? or was he of a famished and restless spirit? He felt his own malady, and longed to ask him some questions about it. But Ambrose could not easily be spoken with. Though accessible to all, yet that very circumstance made it difficult for an individual, especially one who was not of his flock, to get a private interview with him. When he was not taken up with the Christian people who surrounded him, he was either at his meals or engaged in private reading. Augustine used to enter, as all persons might, without being announced; but after staying awhile, afraid of interrupting him, he departed again. However, he heard his expositions of Scripture every Sunday, and gradually made progress.

He was now in his thirtieth year, and since he was a youth of eighteen had been searching after truth; yet he was still "in the same mire, greedy of things present," but finding nothing stable."

To-morrow," he said to himself, "I shall find it; it will appear manifestly, and I shall grasp it: lo, Faustus the Manichee will come and clear everything! O you great men, ye academics, is it true, then, that no certainty can be attained for the ordering of life? Nay, let us search diligently, and despair not. Lo, things in the ecclesiastical books are not absurd to us now, which sometimes seemed absurd, and may be otherwise taken and in a good sense. I will take my stand where, as a child, my parents placed me, until the clear truth be found out. But where shall it be sought, or when? Ambrose has no leisure; we have no leisure to read; where shall we find even the books? where, or when, procure them? Let set times be appointed, and certain hours be ordered for the health of our soul. Great hope has dawned; the Catholic faith teaches not what we thought; and do we doubt to knock, that the rest may be opened? The forenoons, indeed, our scholars take up; what do we during the rest of our time? why not this? But if so, when pay we court to our great friend, whose favors we need? when compose what we may sell to scholars? when refresh ourselves, unbending our minds from this intenseness of care?

"Perish everything: dismiss we these empty vanities; and betake ourselves to the one search for truth! Life is a poor thing, death is uncertain; if it surprises us, in what state shall we depart hence? and when shall we learn what here we have neglected? and shall we not rather suffer the punishment of this negligence? What if death itself cut off and end all care and feeling? Then must this be ascertained. But God forbid this! It is no vain and empty thing, that the excellent dignity of the Christian faith has overspread the whole world. Never would such and so great things be wrought for us by God, if with the body the soul also came to an end. Wherefore delay then to abandon worldly hopes, and give ourselves wholly to seek after God and the blessed life?..."

Finding Ambrose, though kind and accessible, yet reserved, he went to an aged man named Simplician, who, as some say, baptized St. Ambrose, and eventually succeeded him in his see. He opened his mind to him, and happening in the course of his communications to mention Victorinus's translation of some Platonic works, Simplician asked him if he knew that person's history. It seems he was a professor of rhetoric at Rome, was well versed in literature and philosophy, had been tutor to many of the senators, and had received the high honor of a statue in the Forum. Up to his old age he had professed, and defended with his eloquence, the old pagan worship. He was led to read the Holy Scriptures, and was brought, in consequence, to a belief in their divinity. For a while he did not feel the necessity of changing his profession; he looked upon Christianity as a philosophy, he embraced it as such, but did not propose to join what he considered the Christian sect, or, as Christians would call it, the Catholic Church. He let Simplician into his secret; but whenever the latter pressed him to take the step, he was accustomed to ask, "whether walls made a Christian." However, such a state could not continue with a man of earnest mind: the leaven worked; at length he unexpectedly called upon Simplician to lead him to church. He was admitted a catechumen, and in due time baptized, "Rome wondering, the Church rejoicing." It was customary at Rome for the candidates for baptism to profess their faith from a raised place in the church, in a set form of words. An offer was made to Victorinus, which was not unusual in the case of bashful and timid persons, to make his profession in private. But he preferred to make it in the ordinary way. "I was public enough," he made answer, "in my profession of rhetoric, and ought not to be frightened when professing salvation." He continued the school which he had before he became a Christian, till the edict of Julian forced him to close it. This story went to Augustine's heart, but it did not melt it. There was still the struggle of two wills, the high aspiration and the habitual inertness. His conversion took place in the summer of 386.

He gives an account of the termination of the conflict he underwent:

"At length burst forth a mighty storm, bringing a mighty flood of tears; and to indulge it to the full even unto cries, in solitude, I rose up from Alypius, ... who perceived from my choked voice how it was with me. He remained where we had been sitting, in deep astonishment. I threw myself down under a fig tree, I know not how, and allowing my tears full vent, offered up to Thee the acceptable sacrifice of my streaming eyes. And I cried out to this effect: 'And Thou, O Lord, how long, how long, Lord, wilt Thou be angry? Forever? Remember not our old sins!' for I felt that they were my tyrants. I cried out, piteously, 'How long? how long? to-morrow and to-morrow? why not *now*? why not in this very hour put an end to this my vileness?' While I thus spoke, with tears, in the bitter contrition of my heart, suddenly I heard a voice, as if from a house near me, of a boy or girl chanting forth again and again, 'TAKE UP AND READ, TAKE UP AND READ!' Changing countenance at these words, I began intently to think whether boys used them in any game, but could not recollect that I had ever heard them. I left weeping and rose up, considering it a divine intimation to open the Scriptures and read what first presented itself. I had heard that Antony had come in during the reading of the Gospel, and had taken to himself the admonition, 'Go, sell all that thou hast,' etc., and had turned to Thee at once, in consequence of that oracle. I had left St. Paul's volume where Alypius was sitting, when I rose thence. I returned thither, seized it, opened, and read in silence the following passage, which first met my eyes, *'Not in rioting and drunkenness, not in chambering and impurities, not in contention and envy, but put ye on the Lord Jesus Christ, and make not provision for the flesh in its concupiscences.'* I had neither desire nor need to read farther. As I finished the sentence, as though the light of peace had been poured into my heart, all the shadows of doubt dispersed. Thus hast Thou converted me to Thee, so as no longer to

seek either for wife or other hope of this world, standing fast in that
rule of faith in which Thou so many years before hadst revealed me to
my mother."

— VIII. 26-30.

The last words of this extract relate to a dream which his mother
had had some years before, concerning his conversion. On his first
turning Manichee, abhorring his opinions, she would not for a while
even eat with him, when she had this dream, in which she had an intimation that where she stood, there Augustine should one day be with
her. At another time she derived great comfort from the casual words
of a bishop, who, when importuned by her to converse with her son,
said at length with some impatience, "Go thy ways, and God bless
thee, for it is not possible that the son of these tears should perish!"
would be out of place, and is perhaps unnecessary, to enter here into
the affecting and well-known history of her tender anxieties and perse-
vering prayers for Augustine. Suffice it to say, she saw the accomplishment of them; she lived till Augustine became a Catholic; and she died
in her way back to Africa with him. Her last words were, "Lay this
body anywhere; let not the care of it in any way distress you; this only
I ask, that wherever you be, you remember me at the Altar of the
Lord."

"May she," says her son, in dutiful remembrance of her words, "rest in
peace with her husband, before and after whom she never had any;
whom she obeyed, with patience bringing forth fruit unto Thee, that
she might win him also unto Thee. And inspire, O Lord my God,
inspire Thy servants, my brethren,—Thy sons, my masters,—whom, in
heart, voice, and writing I serve, that so many as read these confessions, may at Thy altar remember Monica, Thy handmaid, with Patricius, her sometime husband, from whom Thou broughtest me into this
life; how, I know not. May they with pious affection remember those
who were my parents in this transitory light,—my brethren under
Thee, our Father, in our Catholic Mother,—my fellow-citizens in the
eternal Jerusalem, after which Thy pilgrim people sigh from their going
forth unto their return: that so, her last request of me may in the

prayers of many receive a fulfillment, through my confessions, more abundant than through my prayers."

— IX. 37.

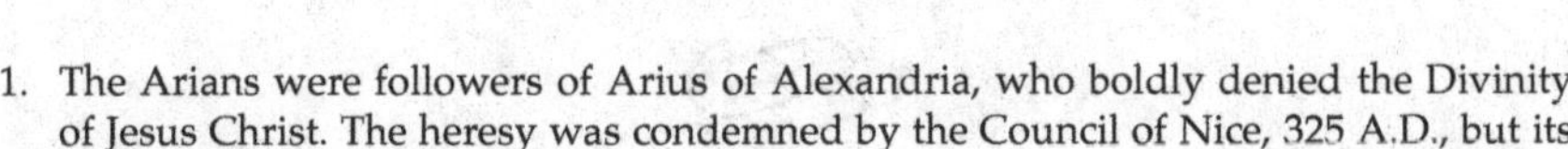

1. The Arians were followers of Arius of Alexandria, who boldly denied the Divinity of Jesus Christ. The heresy was condemned by the Council of Nice, 325 A.D., but its baneful effects were widely felt for centuries.
2. Wonderful revelations made to St. John at Patmos concerning the Church, the final judgment, the future life.
3. A barbarian race of Southern Germany, who in the fifth century ravaged Gaul, Spain, Italy, and Northern Africa.
4. A sect of the second century that believed in Montanus as a prophet, and in the near advent of Christ to judge the world.
5. Ahias.
6. The first king of Israel after the separation of the tribes; a man perverse and irreverent in his relations with God and subject.
7. The apology for flight in times of religious persecution, made by Athanasius, the great bishop of Alexandria, fourth century, and the cogent argument against it of Tertullian, a celebrated writer of the second century, show how circumstances, above all, Divine inspiration, justify opposite lines of action. St. Augustine's letter, written in his strong and luminous style, reconciles the two points of view.
8. A profound analysis of the two classes of men without religion,—the one distorted, brutalized, and deadened; the other confused, wild, and hungering after what is to them indefinable, yet alone satisfying. Compare in its source, tenor, and effect the unhappiness of the "popular poet" Byron and that of Augustine.
9. Most of these translations are from the Oxford edition of 1838.
10. One of the greatest women of all times; a model of faith, constancy, and maternal love.

CHRYSOSTOM

I [1] confess to a delight in reading the lives, and dwelling on the characters and actions, of the Saints of the first ages, such as I receive from none besides them; and for this reason, because we know so much more about them than about most of the Saints who come after them. People are variously constituted; what influences one does not influence another. There are persons of warm imaginations, who can easily picture to themselves what they never saw. They can at will see Angels and Saints hovering over them when they are in church; they see their lineaments, their features, their motions, their gestures, their smile or their grief. They can go home and draw what they have seen, from the vivid memory of what, while it lasted, was so transporting. I am not one of such; I am touched by my five senses, by what my eyes behold and my ears hear. I am touched by what I read about, not by what I myself create. As faith need not lead to practice, so in me mere imagination does not lead to devotion. I gain more from the life of our Lord in the Gospels than from a treatise *de Deo*. I gain more from three verses of St. John than from the three points of a meditation. I like a Spanish crucifix of painted wood more than one from Italy, which is made of gold. I am more touched by the Seven Dolors than by the Immaculate Conception; I am more devout to St. Gabriel than to one of Isaiah's seraphim. I love St. Paul more than one of those first Carmelites, his contemporaries, whose names and acts no one ever heard of; I feel affectionately towards the Alexandrian Dionysius, I do homage to St. George. I do not say that my way is better than another's; but it is my way, and an allowable way. And it is the reason why I am so specially attached to the Saints of the third and fourth century, because we know so much about them. This is why I feel a devout affection for St. Chrysostom. He and the rest of them have written autobiography on a large scale; they have given us their own histories, their thoughts, words, and actions, in a number of goodly folios, productions which are in themselves some of their meritorious works...

The Ancient Saints have left behind them just that kind of literature which more than any other represents the abundance of the heart, which more than any other approaches to conversation; I mean correspondence. Why is it that we feel an interest in Cicero which we cannot feel in Demosthenes or Plato? Plato is the very type of soaring philosophy, and Demosthenes of forcible eloquence; Cicero is something more than an orator and a sage; he is not a mere ideality, he is a man and a brother; he is one of ourselves. We do not merely believe it, or infer it, but we have the enduring and living evidence of it—how? In his letters. He can be studied, criticised if you will; but still dwelt upon and sympathized with also. Now the case of the Ancient Saints is parallel to that of Cicero. We have their letters in a marvelous profusion. We have above 400 letters of St. Basil's; above 200 of St. Augustine's. St. Chrysostom has left us about 240; St. Gregory Nazianzen the same number; Pope St. Gregory as many as 840....

A Saint's writings are to me his real "Life"; and what *is called* his "Life" is not the outline of an individual, but either of the *auto-saint* or of a myth. Perhaps I shall be asked what I mean by "Life." I mean a narrative which impresses the reader with the idea of moral unity, identity, growth, continuity, personality. When a Saint converses with me, I am conscious of the presence of one active principle of thought, one individual character, flowing on and into the various matters which he discusses, and the different transactions in which he mixes. It is what no memorials can reach, however skillfully elaborated, however free from effort or study, however conscientiously faithful, however guaranteed by the veracity of the writers. Why cannot art rival the lily or the rose? Because the colors of the flower are developed and blended by the force of an inward life; while on the other hand, the lights and shades of the painter are diligently laid on from without. A magnifying glass will show the difference. Nor will it improve matters, though not one only, but a dozen good artists successively take part in the picture; even if the outline is unbroken, the coloring is muddy. Commonly, what is called "the Life," is little more than a collection of anecdotes brought together from a number of independent quarters; anecdotes striking, indeed, and edifying, but valuable in themselves rather than valuable as parts of a biography; valuable whoever was the subject of them, not valuable as illustrating a particular Saint. It would be difficult to mistake for each other a paragraph of St. Ambrose, or of St. Jerome, or of St. Augustine; it would be very easy to mistake a chapter in the life of one holy missionary or nun for a chapter in the life of another.

An almsgiving here, an instance of meekness there, a severity of penance, a round of religious duties,—all these things humble me, instruct me, improve me; I cannot desire anything better of their kind; but they do not necessarily coalesce into the image of a person. From such works I do but learn to pay devotion to an abstract and typical perfection under a certain particular name; I do not know more of the real Saint who bore it than before. Saints, as other men, differ from each other in this, that the multitude of qualities which they have in common are differently combined in each of them. This forms one great part of their personality. One Saint is remarkable for fortitude; not that he has not other heroic virtues by *concomitance*, as it may be called, but by virtue of that one gift in particular he has won his crown. Another is remarkable for patient hope, another for renunciation of the world. Such a particular virtue may be said to give form to all the rest which are grouped round it, and are molded and modified by means of it. Thus it is that often what is right in one would be wrong in another; and, in fact, the very same action is allowed or chosen by one, and shunned by another, as being consistent or inconsistent with their respective characters,—pretty much as in the combination of colors, each separate tint takes a shade from the rest, and is good or bad from its company. The whole gives a meaning to the parts; but it is difficult to rise from the parts to the whole. When I read St. Augustine or St. Basil, I hold converse with a beautiful grace-illumined soul, looking out into this world of sense, and leavening it with itself; when I read a professed life of him, I am wandering in a labyrinth of which I cannot find the center and heart, and am but conducted out of doors again when I do my best to penetrate within.

This seems to me, to tell the truth, a sort of pantheistic treatment of the Saints. I ask something more than to stumble upon the *disjecta membra* of what ought to be a living whole. I take but a secondary interest in books which chop up a Saint into chapters of faith, hope, charity, and the cardinal virtues. They are too scientific to be devotional. They have their great utility, but it is not the utility which they profess. They do not manifest a Saint, they mince him into spiritual lessons. They are rightly called spiritual reading, that is just what they are, and they cannot possibly be anything better; but they are not anything else. They contain a series of points of meditation on particular virtues, made easier because those points are put under the patronage and the invocation of a Saint. With a view to learning real devotion to him, I prefer (speaking for myself) to have any one action or event of his life drawn out minutely, with his own comments upon it, than a score of virtues, or of acts of one virtue, strung together in as many sentences. Now, in the ancient writings I have spoken of, certain transactions are thoroughly worked out. We know all that happened to a Saint on such or such an occasion, all that was done by him. We have a view of his character, his tastes, his natural infirmities, his struggles and victories over them, which in no other way can be attained. And therefore it is that, without quarreling with the devotion of others, I give the preference to my own…

Here another great subject opens upon us, when I ought to be bringing these remarks to an end; I mean the endemic perennial fidget which possesses us about giving scandal; facts are omitted in great histories, or glosses are put upon memorable acts, because they are thought not edifying, whereas of all scandals such omissions, such glosses, are the greatest. But I am getting far more argumentative than I thought to be when I began; so I lay my pen down, and retire into myself.

I

John of Antioch, from his sanctity and his eloquence called Chrysostom[2], was approaching sixty years of age, when he had to deliver himself up to the imperial officers, and to leave Constantinople for a distant exile. He had been the great preacher of the day now for nearly twenty years; first at Antioch, then in the metropolis of the East; and his gift of speech, as in the instance of the two great classical orators before him, was to be his ruin. He had made an Empress his enemy, more powerful than Antipater[3],—as passionate, if not so vindictive, as Fulvia[4]. Nor was this all; a zealous Christian preacher offends not individuals merely, but classes of men, and much more so when he is pastor and ruler too, and has to punish as well as to denounce. Eudoxia, the Empress, might be taken off suddenly,—as indeed she was taken off a few weeks after the Saint arrived at the place of exile, which she personally, in spite of his entreaties, had marked out for him; but her death did but serve to increase the violence of the persecution directed against him. She had done her part in it, perhaps she might have even changed her mind in his favor; probably the agitation of a bad conscience was, in her critical condition, the cause of her death. She was taken out of the way; but her partisans, who had made use of her, went on vigorously with the evil work which she had begun. When Cucusus would not kill him, they sent him on his travels anew, across a far wilder country than he had already traversed, to a remote town on the eastern coast of the Euxine; and he sank under this fresh trial.

The Euxine! that strange mysterious sea, which typifies the abyss of outer darkness, as the blue Mediterranean basks under the smile of heaven in the center of civilization and religion. The awful, yet splendid drama of man's history has mainly been carried on upon the Mediterranean shores; while the Black Sea has ever been on the very outskirts of the habitable world, and the scene of wild unnatural portents; with legends of Prometheus on the savage Caucasus, of Medea gathering witch herbs in the moist meadows of the Phasis, and of Iphigenia sacrificing the shipwrecked stranger in Taurica; and then again, with the more historical, yet not more grateful visions of barbarous tribes, Goths, Huns, Scythians, Tartars, flitting over the steppes and wastes which encircle its inhospitable waters. To be driven from the bright cities and sunny clime of Italy or Greece to such a region, was worse than death; and the luxurious Roman actually preferred death to exile. The suicide of Gallus[5], under this dread doom, is well known; Ovid[6], too cowardly to be desperate, drained out the dregs of a vicious life on the cold marshes between the Danube and the sea. I need scarcely allude to the heroic Popes who patiently lived on in the Crimea, till a martyrdom, in which they had not part but the suffering, released them. But banishment was an immense evil in itself. Cicero, even though he had liberty of person, the choice of a home, and the prospect of a return, roamed disconsolate through the cities of Greece, because he was debarred access to the senate-house and forum. Chrysostom had his own *rostra*, his own *curia*; it was the Holy Temple, where his eloquence gained for him victories not less real, and more momentous, than the detection and overthrow of Catiline. Great as was his gift of oratory, it was not by the fertility of his imagination, or the splendor of his diction that he gained the surname of "Mouth of Gold." We shall be very wrong if we suppose that fine expressions, or rounded periods, or figures of speech, were the credentials by which he claimed to be the first doctor of the East. His oratorical power was but the instrument by which he readily, gracefully, adequately expressed—expressed without effort and with felicity—the keen feelings, the living ideas, the earnest practical lessons which he had to communicate to his hearers. He spoke, because his heart, his head, were brimful of things to speak about. His elocution corresponded to that strength and flexibility of limb, that quickness of eye, hand, and foot, by which a man excels in manly games or in mechanical skill. It would be a great mistake, in speaking of it, to ask whether it was Attic or Asiatic, terse or flowing, when its distinctive praise was that it was natural. His unrivaled charm, as that of every really eloquent man, lies in his singleness of purpose, his fixed grasp of his aim, his noble earnestness.

A bright, cheerful, gentle soul; a sensitive heart, a temperament open to emotion and impulse; and all this elevated, refined, transformed by the touch of heaven,—such was St. John Chrysostom; winning followers, riveting affections, by his sweetness, frankness, and neglect of self. In his labors, in his preaching, he thought of others only. "I am always in admiration of that thrice-blessed man," says an able critic,[7] "because he ever in all his writings puts before him as his object, to be useful to his hearers; and as to all other matters, he either simply put them aside, or took the least possible notice of them. Nay, as to his seeming ignorant of some of the thoughts of Scripture, or careless of entering into its depths, and similar defects, all this he utterly disregarded in comparison of the profit of his hearers."

There was as little affectation of sanctity in his dress or living as there was effort in his eloquence. In his youth he had been one of the most austere of men; at the age of twenty-one, renouncing bright prospects of the world, he had devoted himself to prayer and study of the Scriptures. He had retired to the mountains near Antioch, his native place, and had lived among the monks. This had been his home for six years, and he had chosen it in order to subdue the daintiness of his natural appetite. "Lately," he wrote to a friend at the time,—"lately, when I had made up my mind to leave the city and betake myself to the tabernacle of the monks, I was forever inquiring and busying myself how I was to get a supply of provisions; whether it would be possible to procure fresh bread for my eating, whether I should be ordered to use the same oil for my lamp and for my food, to undergo the hardship of peas and beans, or of severe toil, such as digging, carrying wood or water, and the like; in a word, I made much account of bodily comfort."[8] Such was the nervous anxiety and fidget of mind with which he had begun: but this rough discipline soon effected its object, and at length, even by preference, he took upon him mortifications which at first were a trouble to him. For the last two years of his monastic exercise, he lived by himself in a cave; he slept, when he did sleep, without lying down; he exposed himself to the extremities of cold. At length he found he was passing the bounds of discretion, nature would bear no more; he fell ill, and returned to the city.

A course of ascetic practice such as this would leave its spiritual effects upon him for life. It sank deep into him, though the surface might not show it. His duty at Constantinople was to mix with the world; and he lived as others, except as regards such restraints as his sacred office and archiepiscopal station demanded of him. He wore shoes, and an under garment; but his stomach was ever delicate, and at meals he was obliged to have his own dish, such as it was, to himself. However, he mixed freely with all ranks of men; and he made friends, affectionate friends, of young and old, men and women, rich and poor, by condescending to all of every degree. How he was loved at Antioch, is shown by the expedient used to transfer him thence to Constantinople. Asterius, count of the East, had orders to send for him, and ask his company to a church without the city. Having got him into his carriage, he drove off with him to the first station on the highroad to Constantinople, where imperial officers were in readiness to convey him thither. Thus he was brought upon the scene of those trials which have given him a name in history, and a place in the catalogue of the Saints. At the imperial city he was as much followed, if not as popular, as at Antioch. "The people flocked to him," says Sozomen, "as often as he preached; some of them to hear what would profit them, others to make trial of him. He carried them away, one and all, and persuaded them to think as he did about the Divine Nature. They hung upon his words, and could not have enough of them; so that, when they thrust and jammed themselves together in an alarming way, every one making an effort to get nearer to him, and to hear him more perfectly, he took his seat in the midst of them, and taught from the pulpit of the Reader."[9] He was, indeed, a man to make both friends and enemies; to inspire affection, and to kindle resentment; but his friends loved him with a love "stronger" than "death," and more burning than "hell"; and it was well to be so hated, if he was so beloved.

Here he differs, as far as I can judge, from his brother saints and doctors of the Greek Church, St. Basil and St. Gregory Nazianzen. They were scholars, shy perhaps and reserved; and though they had not given up the secular state, they were essentially monks. There is no evidence, that I remember, to show that they attached men to their persons. They, as well as John, had a multitude of enemies; and were regarded, the one with dislike, the other perhaps with contempt; but they had not, on the other hand, warm, eager, sympathetic, indignant, agonized friends. There is another characteristic in Chrysostom, which perhaps gained for him this great blessing. He had, as it would seem, a vigor, elasticity, and, what may be called, sunniness of mind, all his own. He was ever sanguine, seldom sad. Basil had a life-long malady, involving continual gnawing pain and a weight of physical dejection. He bore his burden well and gracefully, like the great Saint he was, as Job bore his; but it was a burden like Job's. He was a calm, mild, grave, autumnal day[10]; St. John Chrysostom was a day in spring-time, bright and rainy, and glittering through its rain. Gregory was the full summer, with a long spell of pleasant stillness, its monotony relieved by thunder and lightning. And St. Athanasius figures to us the stern persecuting winter, with its wild winds, its dreary wastes, its sleep of the great mother, and the bright stars shining overhead. He and Chrysostom have no points in common; but Gregory was a dethroned Archbishop of Constantinople, like Chrysostom, and, again, dethroned by his brethren the Bishops. Like Basil, too, Chrysostom was bowed with infirmities of body; he was often ill; he was thin and wizened; cold was a misery to him; heat affected his head; he scarcely dare touch wine; he was obliged to use the bath; obliged to take exercise, or rather to be continually on the move. Whether from a nervous or febrile complexion, he was warm in temper; or at least, at certain times, his emotion struggled hard with his reason. But he had that noble spirit which complains as little as possible; which makes the best of things; which soon recovers its equanimity, and hopes on in circumstances when others sink down in despair...

II

Whence is this devotion to St. John Chrysostom, which leads me to dwell upon the thought of him, and makes me kindle at his name, when so many other great Saints, as the year brings round their festivals, command indeed my veneration, but exert no personal claim upon my heart? Many holy men have died in exile, many holy men have been successful preachers; and what more can we write upon St. Chrysostom's monument than this, that he was eloquent and that he suffered persecution? He is not an Athanasius, expounding a sacred dogma with a luminousness which is almost an inspiration; nor is he Athanasius, again, in his romantic life-long adventures, in his sublime solitariness, in his ascendancy over all classes of men, in his series of triumphs over material force and civil tyranny. Nor, except by the contrast, does he remind us of that Ambrose who kept his ground obstinately in an imperial city, and fortified himself against the heresy of a court by the living rampart of a devoted population. Nor is he Gregory or Basil, rich in the literature and philosophy of Greece, and embellishing the Church with the spoils of heathenism. Again, he is not an Augustine, devoting long years to one masterpiece of thought, and laying, in successive controversies, the foundations of theology. Nor is he a Jerome, so dead to the world that he can imitate the point and wit of its writers without danger to himself or scandal to his brethren. He has not trampled upon heresy, nor smitten emperors, nor beautified the house or the service of God, nor knit together the portions of Christendom, nor founded a religious order, nor built up the framework of doctrine, nor expounded the science of the Saints; yet I love him, as I love David or St. Paul.

How am I to account for it? It has not happened to me, as it might happen to many a man, that I have devoted time and toil to the study of his writings or of his history, and cry up that upon which I have made an outlay, or love what has become familiar to me. Cases may occur when our admiration for an author is only admiration of our own comments on him, and when our love of an old acquaintance is only our love of old times. For me, I have not written the life of Chrysostom, nor translated his works, nor studied Scripture in his exposition, nor forged weapons of controversy out of his sayings or his doings. Nor is his eloquence of a kind to carry any one away who has ever so little knowledge of the oratory of Greece and Rome. It is not force of words, nor cogency of argument, nor harmony of composition, nor depth or richness of thought, which constitute his power,— whence, then, has he this influence, so mysterious, yet so strong?

I consider St. Chrysostom's charm to lie in his intimate sympathy and compassionateness for the whole world, not only in its strength, but in its weakness; in the lively regard with which he views everything that comes before him, taken in the concrete, whether as made after its own kind or as gifted with a nature higher than its own. Not that any religious man—above all, not that any Saint—could possibly contrive to abstract the love of the work from the love of its Maker, or could feel a tenderness for earth which did not spring from devotion to heaven; or as if he would not love everything just in that degree in which the Creator loves it, and according to the measure of gifts which the Creator has bestowed upon it, and preëminently for the Creator's sake. But this is the characteristic of all Saints; and I am speaking, not of what St. Chrysostom had in common with others, but what he had special to himself; and this specialty, I conceive, is the interest which he takes in all things, not so far as God has made them alike, but as He has made them different from each other. I speak of the discriminating affectionateness[11] with which he accepts every one for what is personal in him and unlike others. I speak of his versatile recognition of men, one by one, for the sake of that portion of good, be it more or less, of a lower order or a higher, which has severally been lodged in them; his eager contemplation of the many things they do, effect, or produce, of all their great works, as nations or as states; nay, even as they are corrupted or disguised by evil, so far as that evil may in imagination be disjoined from their proper nature, or may be regarded as a mere material disorder apart from its formal character of guilt. I speak of the kindly spirit and the genial temper with which he looks round at all things which this wonderful world contains; of the graphic fidelity with which he notes them down upon the tablets of his mind, and of the promptitude and propriety with which he calls them up as arguments or illustrations in the course of his teaching as the occasion requires. Possessed though he be by the fire of Divine charity, he has not lost one fiber, he does not miss one vibration, of the complicated whole of human sentiment and affection; like the miraculous bush in the desert, which, for all the flame that wrapt it round, was not thereby consumed.

Such, in a transcendent perfection, was the gaze, as we may reverently suppose, with which the loving Father of all surveyed in eternity that universe even in its minutest details which He had decreed to create such the loving pity with which He spoke the word when the due moment came, and began to mold the finite, as He created it, in His infinite hands; such the watchful solicitude with which he now keeps His catalogue of the innumerable birds of heaven, and counts day by day the very hairs of our head and the alternations of our breathing. Such, much more, is the awful contemplation with which He encompasses incessantly every one of those souls on whom He heaps His mercies here, in order to make them the intimate associates of His own eternity hereafter. And we too, in our measure, are bound to imitate Him in our exact and vivid apprehension of Himself and of His works. As to Himself, we love Him, not simply in His nature, but in His triple personality, lest we become mere pantheists. And so, again, we choose our patron Saints, not for what they have in common with each other (else there could be no room for choice at all), but for what is peculiar to them severally. That which is my warrant, therefore, for particular devotions at all, becomes itself my reason for devotion to St. John Chrysostom. In him I recognize a special pattern of that very gift of discrimination. He may indeed be said in some sense to have a devotion of his own for every one who comes across him,—for persons, ranks, classes, callings, societies, considered as Divine works and the subjects of his good offices or good will, and therefore I have a devotion for him.

It is this observant benevolence which gives to his exposition of Scripture its chief characteristic. He is known in ecclesiastical literature as the expounder, above all others, of its literal sense. Now in mystical comments the direct object which the writer sets before him is the Divine Author Himself of the written Word. Such a writer sees in Scripture, not so much the works of God, as His nature and attributes; the Teacher more than the definite teaching, or its human instruments, with their drifts and motives, their courses of thought, their circumstances and personal peculiarities. He loses the creature in the glory which surrounds the Creator. The problem before him is not what the inspired writer directly meant, and why, but, out of the myriad of meanings present to the Infinite Being who inspired him, which it is that is most illustrative of that Great Being's all-holy attributes and solemn dispositions. Thus, in the Psalter, he will drop David and Israel and the Temple together, and will recognize nothing there but the shadows of those greater truths which remain forever. Accordingly, the mystical comment will be of an objective character; whereas a writer who delights to ponder human nature and human affairs, to analyze the workings of the mind, and to contemplate what is subjective to it, is naturally drawn to investigate the sense of the sacred writer himself, who was the organ of the revelation, that is, he will investigate the literal sense. Now, in the instance of St. Chrysostom, it so happens that literal exposition is the historical characteristic of the school in which he was brought up; so that if he commented on Scripture at all, he anyhow would have adopted that method; still, there have been many literal expositors, but only one Chrysostom. It is St. Chrysostom who is the charm of the method, not the method that is the charm of St. Chrysostom.

That charm lies, as I have said, in his habit and his power of throwing himself into the minds of others, of imagining with exactness and with sympathy circumstances or scenes which were not before him, and of bringing out what he has apprehended in words as direct and vivid as the apprehension. His page is like the table of a *camera lucida*, which represents to us the living action and interaction of all that goes on around us. That loving scrutiny, with which he follows the Apostles as they reveal themselves to us in their writings, he practices in various ways towards all men, living and dead, high and low, those whom he admires and those whom he weeps over. He writes as one who was ever looking out with sharp but kind eyes upon the world of men and their history; and hence he has always something to produce about them, new or old, to the purpose of his argument, whether from books or from the experience of life. Head and heart were full to over-flowing with a stream of mingled "wine and milk," of rich vigorous thought and affectionate feeling. This is why his manner of writing is so rare and special; and why, when once a student enters into it, he will ever recognize him, wherever he meets with extracts from him.

Letters of Chrysostom[12], written in Exile"To Olympias

"Why do you bewail me? Why beat your breast, and abandon your-self to the tyranny of despondency? Why are you grieved because you have failed in effecting my removal from Cucusus[13]? Yet, as far as your own part is concerned, you have effected it, since you have left nothing undone in attempting it. Nor have you any reason to grieve for your ill success; perhaps it has seemed good to God to make my race course longer that my crown may be brighter. You ought to leap and dance and crown yourself for this, viz., that I should be accounted worthy of so great a matter, which far exceeds my merit. Does my present loneli-ness distress you? On the contrary, what can be more pleasant than my sojourn here? I have quiet, calm, much leisure, excellent health. To be sure, there is no market in the city, nor anything on sale; but this does not affect me; for all things, as if from some fountains, flow in upon me. Here is my lord, the Bishop of the place, and my lord Dioscorus, making it their sole business to make me comfortable. That excellent person Patricius will tell you in what good spirits and lightness of mind, and amid what kind attentions, I am passing my time."

— EP. 14.

The same is his report to his friends at Cæesarea, and the same are his expressions of gratitude and affection towards them. The following is addressed to the President of Cappodocia:

"To Carterius

"Cucusus is a place desolate in the extreme; however, it does not annoy
me so much by its desolateness as it relieves me by its quiet and its
leisure. Accordingly, I have found a sort of harbor in this desolateness;
and have set me down to recover breath after the miseries of the journey, and have availed myself of the quiet to dispose of what remained
both of my illness and of the other troubles which I have undergone. I
say this to your illustriousness, knowing well the joy you feel in this
rest of mine. I can never forget what you did for me in Cæsarea, in
quelling those furious and senseless tumults, and striving to the
utmost, as far as your powers extended, to place me in security. I give
this out publicly wherever I go, feeling the liveliest gratitude to you,
my most worshipful lord, for so great solicitude towards me."

— EP. 236.

"To Diogenes

"Cucusus is indeed a desolate spot, and moreover unsafe to dwell in,
from the continual danger to which it is exposed of brigands. You,
however, though away, have turned it for me into a paradise. For, when
I hear of your abundant zeal and charity in my behalf, so genuine and
warm (it does not at all escape me, far removed as I am from you), I
possess a great treasure and untold wealth in such affection, and feel
myself to be dwelling in the safest of cities, by reason of the great gladness which bears me up, and the high consolation which I enjoy."

— EP. 144.

Diogenes was one of the friends who sent him supplies: he writes
in answer:

"You know very well yourself that I have ever been one of your most
warmly attached admirers; therefore I beg you will not be hurt at my
having returned your presents. I have pressed out of them and have
quaffed the honor which they did me; and if I return the things themselves, it has been from no slight or distrust of you, but because I was

in no need of them. I have done the same in the case of many others;
for many others too, with a generosity like yours, ardent friends of
mine, have made me the same offers; and the same apology has set me
right with them which I now ask you to receive. If I am in want, I will
ask these things of you with much freedom, as if they were my own
property, nay with more, as the event will show. Receive them back,
then, and keep them carefully; so that, if there is a call for them some
time hence, I may reckon on them."

— EP. 50.

As a fellow to the above, I add one of his letters:

"To Carteria

"What are you saying? that your unintermitting ailments have
hindered you from visiting me? but you *have* come, you are present
with me. From your very intention I have gained all this, nor have you
any need to excuse yourself in this matter. That warm and true charity
of yours, so vigorous, so constant, suffices to make me very happy.
What I have ever declared in my letters, I now declare again, that,
wherever I may be, though I be transported to a still more desolate
place than this, you and your matters I never shall forget. Such pledges
of your warm and true charity have you stored up for me, pledges
which length of time can never obliterate nor waste; but, whether I am
near you or far away, ever do I cherish that same charity, being assured
of the loyalty and sincerity of your affection for me, which has been my
comfort hitherto."

— EP. 227.

"To Olympias

"It is not a light effort," he says (*Ep.* 2), "but it demands an energetic
soul and a great mind to bear separation from one whom we love in
the charity of Christ. Every one knows this who knows what it is to
love sincerely, who knows the power of supernatural love. Take the
blessed Paul: here was a man who had stripped himself of the flesh,

and who went about the world almost with a disembodied soul, who had exterminated from his heart every wild impulse, and who imitated the passionless sereneness of the immaterial intelligences, and who stood on high with the Cherubim, and shared with them in their mystical music, and bore prisons, chains, transportations, scourges, stoning, shipwreck, and every form of suffering; yet he, when separated from one soul loved by him in Christian charity, was so confounded and distracted as all at once to rush out of that city, in which he did not find the beloved one whom he expected. 'When I was come to Troas[14],' he says, 'for the gospel of Christ, and a door was opened to me in the Lord, I had no rest in my spirit, because I found not Titus my brother; but bidding them farewell, I went into Macedonia.'

"Is it Paul who says this?" he continues; "Paul who, even when fastened in the stocks, when confined in a dungeon, when torn with the bloody scourge, did nevertheless convert and baptize and offer sacrifice, and was chary even of one soul which was seeking salvation? and now, when he has arrived at Troas, and sees the field cleansed of weeds, and ready for the sowing, and the floor full, and ready to his hand, suddenly he flings away the profit, though he came thither expressly for it. 'So it was,' he answers me, 'just so; I was possessed by a predominating tyranny of sorrow, for Titus was away; and this so wrought upon me as to compel me to this course.' Those who have the grace of charity are not content to be united in soul only, they seek for the personal presence of him they love. "Turn once more to this scholar of charity, and you will find that so it is. 'We, brethren,' he says, 'being bereaved of you for the time of an hour, in sight, not in heart, have hastened the more abundantly to see your face with great desire. For we would have come unto you, I, Paul, indeed, once and again, but Satan hath hindered us. For which cause, forbearing no longer, we thought it good to remain at Athens alone, and we sent Timothy.' What force is there in each expression! That flame of charity living in his soul is manifested with singular luminousness. He does not say so much as 'separated from you,' nor 'torn,' nor 'divided,' nor 'abandoned,' but only 'bereaved'; moreover not 'for a certain period,' but merely 'for the time of an hour'; and separated, 'not in heart, but in presence only'; again, 'have hastened the more abundantly to see your face.' What! it seems charity so captivated you that you desiderated their sight, you longed to gaze upon{ their earthly, fleshly countenance? 'Indeed I did,' he answers: 'I am not ashamed to say so; for in that seeing all the channels of the senses meet together. I desire to see your presence; for there is the tongue which utters sounds and announces the secret feelings; there is the hearing which receives words, and there the eyes which image the movements of the soul.' But this is not all: not content with writing to them letters, he actually sends to them Timothy, who was with him, and who was more than any letters. And, 'We thought it good to remain alone;' that is, when he is divided from one brother, he says, he is left alone, though he had so many others with him."

---

1. The personal touch of these pages gives an insight into the tender, sensitive nature of Cardinal Newman. He was a man not only of intense and powerful intellect, but of delicate and affectionate heart. It is his gracious, winning appeal that renders him irresistible in influence.
2. "Golden mouth," from his eloquence. He is counted among the great Patristic writers.
3. Son of Herod the Great; called by Josephus "a monster of iniquity." He was put to death, 1 B.C.
4. Wife of Marc Antony; noted for her cruelty and ambition.
5. Governor of Egypt under Augustus; accused of crime and oppression, and banished.
6. A celebrated Roman poet, author of *Metamorphoses*; exiled by Augustus for some grave offense never revealed.
7. Photius, p. 387.
8. Ad Demetrium, i. 6.
9. Hist. viii. 5.
10. This apt and ingenious analogy is regarded as one of Newman's more beautiful passages.
11. The reason, probably, why he has so great a hold upon the heart of posterity—love begets love.
12. The charm of his genius, the sweetness of his temper under suffering, and the unselfishness of his lofty soul appear in these simple lines written on the road or in the desert of his banishment.
13. In Caucasus, east of the Black Sea and north of Persia.
14. In Northwest Asia Minor. Troad contains ancient Troy.

PART II
THE TURK

THE TARTAR AND THE TURK

*Y*ou may think, Gentlemen, I have been very long in coming to the Turks[1], and indeed I have been longer than I could have wished; but I have thought it necessary, in order to your taking a just view of them, that you should survey them first of all in their original condition. When they first appear in history they are Huns or Tartars[2], and nothing else; they are indeed in no unimportant respects Tartars even now; but, had they never been made something more than Tartars, they never would have had much to do with the history of the world. In that case, they would have had only the fortunes of Attila[3] and Zingis[4]; they might have swept over the face of the earth, and scourged the human race, powerful to destroy, helpless to construct, and in consequence ephemeral; but this would have been all. But this has not been all, as regards the Turks; for, in spite of their intimate resemblance or relationship to the Tartar tribes, in spite of their essential barbarism to this day, still they, or at least great portions of the race, have been put under education; they have been submitted to a slow course of change, with a long history and a profitable discipline and fortunes of a peculiar kind; and thus they have gained those qualities of mind, which alone enable a nation to wield and to consolidate imperial power.

I have said that, when first they distinctly appear on the scene of history, they are indistinguishable from Tartars. Mount Altai, the high metropolis of Tartary, is surrounded by a hilly district, rich not only in the useful, but in the precious metals. Gold is said to abound there; but it is still more fertile in veins of iron, which indeed is said to be the most plentiful in the world. There have been iron works there from time immemorial, and at the time that the Huns descended on the Roman Empire (in the fifth century of the Christian era), we find the Turks nothing more than a family of slaves, employed as workers of the ore and as blacksmiths by the dominant tribe. Suddenly in the course of fifty years, soon after the fall of the Hunnish power in Europe, with the sudden development peculiar to Tartars, we find these Turks spread from East to West, and lords of a territory so extensive, that they were connected, by relations of peace or war, at once with the Chinese, the Persians, and the Romans. They had reached Kamtchatka on the North, the Caspian on the West, and perhaps even the mouth of the Indus on the South. Here then we have an intermediate empire of Tartars, placed between the eras of Attila and Zingis; but in this sketch it has no place, except as belonging to Turkish history, because it was contained within the limits of Asia, and, though it lasted for 200 years, it only faintly affected the political transactions of Europe. However, it was not without some sort of influence on Christendom, for the Romans interchanged embassies with its sovereign in the reign of the then Greek Emperor Justin the younger (A.D. 570), with the view of engaging him in a warlike alliance against Persia. The account of one of these embassies remains, and the picture it presents of the Turks is important, because it seems clearly to identify them with the Tartar race.

For instance, in the mission to the Tartars from the Pope, which I have already spoken of, the friars were led between two fires, when they approached the Khan, and they at first refused to follow, thinking they might be countenancing some magical rite. Now we find it recorded of this Roman embassy, that, on its arrival, it was purified by the Turks with fire and incense. As to incense, which seems out of place among such barbarians, it is remarkable that it is used in the ceremonial of the Turkish court to this day. At least Sir Charles Fellows, in his work on the Antiquities of Asia Minor, in 1838, speaks of the Sultan as going to the festival of Bairam with incense-bearers before him. Again, when the Romans were presented to the great

Khan, they found him in his tent, seated on a throne, to which wheels were attached and horses attachable, in other words, a Tartar wagon. Moreover, they were entertained at a banquet which lasted the greater part of the day; and an intoxicating liquor, not wine, which was sweet and pleasant, was freely presented to them; evidently the Tartar *koumiss*.[5] The next day they had a second entertainment in a still more splendid tent; the hangings were of embroidered silk, and the throne, the cups, and the vases were of gold. On the third day, the pavilion, in which they were received, was supported on gilt columns; a couch of massive gold was raised on four gold peacocks; and before the entrance to the tent was what might be called a sideboard, only that it was a sort of barricade of wagons, laden with dishes, basins, and statues of solid silver. All these points in the description—the silk hangings, the gold vessels, the successively increasing splendor of the entertainments—remind us of the courts of Zingis and Timour[6], 700 and 900 years afterwards.

This empire, then, of the Turks was of a Tartar character; yet it was the first step of their passing from barbarism to that degree of civilization which is their historical badge. And it was their first step in civilization, not so much by what it did in its day, as (unless it be a paradox to say so) by its coming to an end. Indeed it so happens, that those Turkish tribes which have changed their original character and have a place in the history of the world, have obtained their *status* and their qualifications for it, by a process very different from that which took place in the nations most familiar to us. What this process has been I will say presently; first, however, let us observe that, fortunately for our purpose, we have still specimens existing of those other Turkish tribes, which were never submitted to this process of education and change, and, in looking at them as they now exist, we see at this very day the Turkish nationality in something very like its original form, and are able to decide for ourselves on its close approximation to the Tartar. You may recollect I pointed out to you, Gentlemen, in the opening of these lectures, the course which the pastoral tribes, or nomads as they are often called, must necessarily take in their emigrations. They were forced along in one direction till they emerged from their mountain valleys, and descended their high plateau at the end of Tartary, and then they had the opportunity of turning south. If they did not avail themselves of this opening, but went on still westward, their next southern pass would be the defiles of the Caucasus and Circassia, to the west of the Caspian. If they did not use this, they would skirt the top of the Black Sea, and so reach Europe. Thus in the emigration of the Huns from China, you may recollect a tribe of them turned to the South as soon as they could, and settled themselves between the high Tartar land and the sea of Aral, while the main body went on to the furthest West by the north of the Black Sea. Now with this last passage into Europe we are not here concerned, for the Turks have never introduced themselves to Europe by means of it;[7] but with those two southward passages which are Asiatic, viz., that to the east of the Aral, and that to the west of the Caspian. The Turkish tribes have all descended upon the civilized world by one or other of these two roads; and I observe, that those which have descended along the east of the Aral have changed their social habits and gained political power, while those which descended to the west of the Caspian remain pretty much what they ever were. The former of these go among us by the general name of Turks; the latter are the Turcomans or Turkmans.... At the very date at which Heraclius[8] called the Turcomans into Georgia, at the very date when their Eastern brethren crossed the northern border of Sogdiana, an event of most momentous import had occurred in the South. A new religion had arisen in Arabia. The impostor Mahomet, announcing himself the Prophet of God, was writing the pages of that book[9], and molding the faith of that people, which was to subdue half the known world. The Turks passed the Jaxartes southward in A.D. 626; just four years before Mahomet had assumed the royal dignity, and just six years after, on his death, his followers began the conquest of the Persian Empire. In the course of 20 years they effected it; Sogdiana was at its very extremity, or its borderland; there the last king of Persia took refuge from the south, while the Turks were pouring into it from the north. There was little to choose for the unfortunate prince between the Turk and the Saracen; the Turks were his hereditary foe; they had been the giants and monsters of the popular poetry; but he threw himself into their arms. They engaged in his service, betrayed him, murdered him, and measured themselves with the Saracens in his stead. Thus the military strength of the north and south of Asia, the Saracenic and the Turkish, came into memorable conflict in the regions of which I have said so much. The struggle was a fierce one, and lasted many years; the Turks striving to force their way down to the ocean, the Saracens to drive them back into their Scythian deserts. They first fought this issue in Bactriana or Khorasan; the Turks got the worst of the fight, and then it was thrown back upon Sogdiana itself, and there it ended again in favor of the Saracens. At the end of 90 years from the time of the first Turkish descent on this fair region, they relinquished it to their Mahometan opponents. The conquerors found it rich, populous, and powerful; its cities, Carisme, Bokhara, and Samarcand, were surrounded beyond their fortifications by a suburb of fields and gardens, which was in turn protected by exterior works; its plains were well cultivated, and its commerce extended from China to Europe. Its riches were proportionally great; the Saracens were able to extort a tribute of two million gold pieces from the inhabitants; we read, moreover, of the crown jewels of one of the Turkish princesses; and of the buskin of another, which she dropt in her flight from Bokhara, as being worth two thousand pieces of gold.[10] Such had been the prosperity of the barbarian invaders, such was its end; but not *their* end, for adversity did them service, as well as prosperity, as we shall see.

It is usual for historians to say, that the triumph of the South threw the Turks back again upon their northern solitudes; and this might easily be the case with some of the many hordes, which were ever passing the boundary and flocking down; but it is no just account of the historical fact, viewed as a whole. Not often indeed do the Oriental nations present us with an example of versatility of character; the Turks, for instance, of this day are substantially what they were four centuries ago. We cannot conceive, were Turkey overrun by the Russians at the present moment, that the fanatical tribes, which are pouring into Constantinople from Asia Minor, would submit to the foreign yoke, take service under their conquerors, become soldiers, custom-officers, police, men of business, attaches, statesmen, working their way up from the ranks and from the masses into influence and power; but, whether from skill in the Saracens, or from far-reaching sagacity in the Turks (and it is difficult to assign it to either cause), so it was, that a process of this nature followed close upon the Mahometan conquest of Sogdiana. It is to be traced in detail to a variety of accidents. Many of the Turks probably were made slaves, and the service to which they were subjected was no matter of choice. Numbers had got attached to the soil; and inheriting the blood of Persians, White Huns, or aboriginal inhabitants for three generations, had simply unlearned the wildness of the Tartar shepherd. Others fell victims to the religion of their conquerors, which ultimately, as we know, exercised a most remarkable influence upon them. Not all at once, but as tribe descended after tribe, and generation followed generation, they succumbed to the creed of Mahomet; and they embraced it with the ardor and enthusiasm which Franks and Saxons so gloriously and meritoriously manifested in their conversion to Christianity.

Here again was a very powerful instrument in modification of their national character. Let me illustrate it in one particular. If there is one peculiarity above another, proper to the savage and to the Tartar, it is that of excitability and impetuosity on ordinary occasions; the Turks, on the other hand, are nationally remarkable for gravity and almost apathy of demeanor. Now there are evidently elements in the Mahometan creed, which would tend to change them from the one temperament to the other. Its sternness, its coldness, its doctrine of fatalism; even the truths which it borrowed from Revelation, when separated from the truths it rejected, its monotheism untempered by mediation[11], its severe view of the Divine attributes, of the law, and of a sure retribution to come, wrought both a gloom and also an improvement in the barbarian, not very unlike the effect which some forms of Protestantism produce among ourselves. But whatever was the mode of operation, certainly it is to their religion that this peculiarity of the Turks is ascribed by competent judges. Lieutenant Wood in his journal gives us a lively account of a peculiarity of theirs, which he unhesitatingly attributes to Islamism. "Nowhere," he says, "is the difference between European and Mahometan society more strongly marked than in the lower walks of life.... A Kasid, or messenger, for example, will come into a public department, deliver his letters in full durbar[12], and demean himself throughout the interview with so much composure and self-possession, that an European can hardly believe that his grade in society is so low. After he has delivered his letters, he takes his seat among the crowd, and answers, calmly and without hesitation, all the questions which may be addressed to him, or communicates the verbal instructions with which he has been intrusted by his employer, and which are often of more importance than the letters themselves. Indeed, all the inferior classes possess an innate self-respect, and a natural gravity of deportment, which differs as far from the suppleness of a Hindustani as from the awkward rusticity of an English clown." ... "Even children," he continues, "in Mahometan countries have an unusual degree of gravity in their deportment. The boy, who can but lisp his 'Peace be with you,' has imbibed this portion of the national character. In passing through a village, these little men will place their hands upon their breasts, and give the usual greeting. Frequently have I seen the children of chiefs approach their father's durbar, and stopping short at the threshold of the door, utter the shout of 'Salam Ali-Kum,' so as to draw all eyes upon them; but nothing daunted, they marched boldly into the room, and sliding down upon their knees, folded their arms and took their seat upon the musnad with all the gravity of grown-up persons."

As Islamism has changed the demeanor of the Turks, so doubtless it has in other ways materially innovated on their Tartar nature. It has given an aim to their military efforts, a political principle, and a social bond. It has laid them under a sense of responsibility, has molded them into consistency, and taught them a course of policy and perseverance in it. But to treat this part of the subject adequately to its importance would require, Gentlemen, a research and a fullness of discussion unsuitable to the historical sketch which I have undertaken. I have said enough for my purpose upon this topic; and indeed on the general question of the modification of national character to which the Turks were at this period subjected.

---

1. **Introductory Note.** These sketches of Turkish history form the substance of lectures delivered in Liverpool, 1853. Special interest attached to them at the time, as England was about to undertake the defense of the Turks against Russia in the Crimean War. Selections from only three are here possible.
2. Fierce, restless tribes originally inhabiting Manchuria and Mongolia.
3. Leader of the Huns, who overran Southern Europe in the fifth century. He was defeated by Aëtius at Chalons, 451, and miraculously turned from Rome by Pope Leo the Great.
4. Zenghis Khan, a powerful Mongol chief whose hordes descended upon Eastern Europe in the thirteenth century.
5. Univ. Hist. Modern, vol. iii. p. 346.
6. Known as Tamerlane, founder of a Mongol empire in Central Asia; victor over Bajazet at Angora, 1402 A.D.
7. I am here assuming that the Magyars are not of the Turkish stock; vid. Gibbon and Pritchard.
8. Emperor of Greece in the seventh century; noted for his rescue of the true Cross from the Persians, with whom he waged long wars.

9. The Koran or bible of the Mahometans. It is a mixture of Judaism, Nestorianism, and Mahomet's own so-called "revelations.

10. Gibbon.

11. Belief in one God, but denial of the Redemption of fallen man by Jesus Christ, the God-Man.

12. A levee held by a dignitary in British India; also the room of reception.

THE TURK AND THE SARACEN

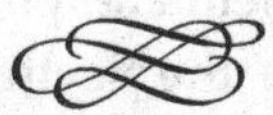

$\mathcal{M}$ere occupation of a rich country is not enough for civilization, as I have granted already. The Turks came into the pleasant plains and valleys of Sogdiana; the Turcomans into the well-wooded mountains and sunny slopes of Asia Minor. The Turcomans were brought out of their dreary deserts, yet they retained their old habits, and they remain barbarians to this day. But why? it must be borne in mind, they neither subjugated the inhabitants of their new country on the one hand, nor were subjugated by them on the other. They never had direct or intimate relations with it; they were brought into it by the Roman Government at Constantinople as its auxiliaries, but they never naturalized themselves there. They were like gypsies in England, except that they were mounted freebooters instead of pilferers and fortune tellers. It was far otherwise with their brethren in Sogdiana; they were there first as conquerors, then as conquered. First they held it in possession as their prize for 90 or 100 years; they came into the usufruct and enjoyment of it. Next, their political ascendancy over it involved, as in the case of the White Huns[1], some sort of moral surrender of themselves to it. What was the first consequence of this? that, like the White Huns, they intermarried with the races they found there. We know the custom of the Tartars and Turks; under such circumstances they would avail themselves of their national practice of polygamy to its full extent of license. In the course of twenty years a new generation would arise of a mixed race; and these in turn would marry into the native population, and at the end of ninety or a hundred years we should find the great-grandsons or the great-great-grandsons of the wild marauders who first crossed the Jaxartes, so different from their ancestors in features both of mind and body, that they hardly would be recognized as deserving the Tartar name. At the end of that period their power came to an end, the Saracens[2] became masters of them and of their country, but the process of emigration southward from the Scythian desert, which had never intermitted during the years of their domination, continued still, though that domination was no more.

Here it is necessary to have a clear idea of the nature of that association of the Turkish tribes from the Volga to the Eastern Sea, to which I have given the name of Empire: it was not so much of a political as of a national character; it was the power, not of a system, but of a race. They were not one well-organized state, but a number of independent tribes, acting generally together, acknowledging one leader or not, according to circumstances, combining and coöperating from the identity of object which acted on them, and often jealous of each other and quarreling with each other on account of that very identity. Each tribe made its way down to the south as it could; one blocked up the way of the other for a time; there were stoppages and collisions, but there was a continual movement and progress. Down they came one after another, like wolves after their prey; and as the tribes which came first became partially civilized, and as a mixed generation arose, these would naturally be desirous of keeping back their less polished uncles or cousins, if they could; and would do so successfully for a while: but cupidity is stronger than conservatism; and so, in spite of delay and difficulty, down they would keep coming, and down they did come, even after and in spite of the overthrow of their Empire; crowding down as to a new world, to get what they could, as adventurers, ready to turn to the right or the left, prepared to struggle on anyhow, willing to be forced forward into countries farther still, careless what might turn up, so that they did but get down. And this was the process which went on (whatever were their fortunes when they actually got down, prosperous or adverse) for 400, nay, I will say for 700 years. The storehouse of the north was never exhausted; it sustained the never ending run upon its resources.

I was just now referring to a change in the Turks, which I have mentioned before, and which had as important a bearing as any other of their changes upon their subsequent fortunes. It was a change in their physiognomy and shape, so striking as to recommend them to their masters for the purposes of war or of display. Instead of bearing any longer the hideous exterior which in the Huns frightened the Romans and Goths, they were remarkable, even as early as the ninth century, when they had been among the natives of Sogdiana[3] only two hundred years, for the beauty of their persons. An important political event was the result: hence the introduction of the Turks into the heart of the Saracenic empire. By this time the Caliphs had removed from Damascus[4] to Bagdad; Persia was the imperial province, and into Persia they were introduced for the reason I have mentioned, sometimes as slaves, sometimes as captives taken in war, sometimes as mercenaries for the Saracenic armies: at length they were enrolled as guards to the Caliph, and even appointed to offices in the palace, to the command of the forces, and to governorships in the provinces. The son of the celebrated Harun al Raschid[5] had as many as 50,000 of these troops in Bagdad itself. And thus slowly and silently they made their way to the south, not with the pomp and pretense of conquest, but by means of that ordinary inter-communion which connected one portion of the empire of the Caliphs with another. In this manner they were introduced even into Egypt.

This was their history for a hundred and fifty years, and what do we suppose would be the result of this importation of barbarians into the heart of a nourishing empire? Would they be absorbed as slaves or settlers in the mass of the population, or would they, like mercenaries elsewhere, be fatal to the power that introduced them? The answer is not difficult, considering that their very introduction argued a want of energy and resource in the rulers whom they served. To employ them was a confession of weakness; the Saracenic power indeed was not very aged, but the Turkish was much younger, and more vigorous; then too must be considered the difference of national character between the Turks and the Saracens. A writer of the beginning of the present century[6] compares the Turks to the Romans; such parallels are generally fanciful and fallacious; but, if we must accept it in the present instance, we may complete the picture by likening the Saracens and Persians to the Greeks, and we know what was the result of the collision between Greece and Rome. The Persians were poets, the Saracens were philosophers. The mathematics, astronomy, and botany were especial subjects of the studies of the latter. Their observatories were celebrated, and they may be considered to have originated the science of chemistry. The Turks, on the other hand, though they are said to have a literature, and though certain of their princes have been patrons of letters, have never distinguished themselves in exercises of pure intellect; but they have had an energy of character, a pertinacity, a perseverance, and a political talent, in a word, they then had the qualities of mind necessary for ruling, in far greater measure, than the people they were serving. The Saracens, like the Greeks, carried their arms over the surface of the earth with an unrivaled brilliancy and an uncheckered success; but their dominion, like that of Greece, did not last for more than 200 or 300 years. Rome grew slowly through many centuries, and its influence lasts to this day; the Turkish race battled with difficulties and reverses, and made its way on amid tumult and complication, for a good 1000 years from first to last, till at length it found itself in possession of Constantinople, and a terror to the whole of Europe. It has ended its career[7] upon the throne of Constantine; it began it as the slave and hireling of the rulers of a great empire, of Persia and Sogdiana.

As to Sogdiana, we have already reviewed one season of power and then in turn of reverse which there befell the Turks; and next a more remarkable outbreak and its reaction mark their presence in Persia. I have spoken of the formidable force, consisting of Turks, which formed the guard of the Caliphs immediately after the time of Harun al Raschid: suddenly they rebelled against their master, burst into his apartment at the hour of supper, murdered him, and cut his body into seven pieces. They got possession of the symbols of imperial power, the garment and the staff of Mahomet, and proceeded to make and unmake Caliphs at their pleasure. In the course of four years they had elevated, deposed, and murdered as many as three. At their wanton caprice, they made these successors of the false prophet the sport of their insults and their blows. They dragged them by the feet, stripped them, and exposed them to the burning sun, beat them with iron clubs, and left them for days without food. At length, however, the people of Bagdad were roused in defense of the Caliphate, and the Turks for a time were brought under; but they remained in the country, or rather, by the short-sighted policy of the moment, were dispersed throughout it, and thus became in the sequel ready-made elements of revolution for the purposes of other traitors of their own race, who, at a later period, as we shall presently see, descended on Persia from Turkistan.

Indeed, events were opening the way slowly, but surely, to their ascendancy. Throughout the whole of the tenth century, which followed, they seem to disappear from history; but a silent revolution was all along in progress, leading them forward to their great destiny. The empire of the Caliphate was already dying in its extremities, and Sogdiana was one of the first countries to be detached from his power. The Turks were still there, and, as in Persia, filled the ranks of the army and the offices of the government; but the political changes which took place were not at first to their visible advantage. What first occurred was the revolt of the Caliph's viceroy, who made himself a great kingdom or empire out of the provinces around, extending it from the Jaxartes, which was the northern boundary of Sogdiana, almost to the Indian Ocean, and from the confines of Georgia to the mountains of Afghanistan. The dynasty thus established lasted for four generations and for the space of ninety years. Then the successor happened to be a boy; and one of his servants, the governor of Khorasan[8], an able and experienced man, was forced by circumstances to rebellion against him. He was successful, and the whole power of this great kingdom fell into his hands; now he was a Tartar or Turk; and thus at length the Turks suddenly appear in history, the acknowledged masters of a southern dominion.

This is the origin of the celebrated Turkish dynasty of the Gaznevides, so called after Gazneh, or Ghizni, or Ghuznee, the principal city, and it lasted for two hundred years. We are not particularly concerned in it, because it has no direct relations with Europe; but it falls into our subject, as having been instrumental to the advance of the Turks towards the West. Its most distinguished monarch was Mahmood, and he conquered Hindostan, which became eventually the seat of the empire. In Mahmood the Gaznevide we have a prince of true Oriental splendor. For him the title of Sultan or Soldan was invented, which henceforth became the special badge of the Turkish monarchs; as Khan is the title of the sovereign of the Tartars, and Caliph of the sovereign of the Saracens. I have already described generally the extent of his dominions: he inherited Sogdiana, Carisme, Khorasan, and Cabul; but, being a zealous Mussulman, he obtained the title of Gazi, or champion, by his reduction of Hindostan, and his destruction of its idol temples. There was no need, however, of religious enthusiasm to stimulate him to the war: the riches, which he amassed in the course of it, were a recompense amply sufficient. His Indian expeditions in all amounted to twelve, and they abound in battles and sieges of a truly Oriental cast....

We have now arrived at what may literally be called the turning point of Turkish history. We have seen them gradually descend from the north, and in a certain degree become acclimated in the countries where they settled. They first appear across the Jaxartes in the beginning of the seventh century; they have now come to the beginning of the eleventh. Four centuries or thereabout have they been out of their deserts, gaining experience and educating themselves in such measure as was necessary for playing their part in the civilized world. First they came down into Sogdiana and Khorasan, and the country below it, as conquerors; they continued in it as subjects and slaves. They offered their services to the race which had subdued them; they made their way by means of their new masters down to the west and the south; they laid the foundations for their future supremacy in Persia, and gradually rose upwards through the social fabric to which they had been admitted, till they found themselves at length at the head of it. The sovereign power which they had acquired in the line of the Gaznevides, drifted off to Hindostan; but still fresh tribes of their race poured down from the north, and filled up the gap; and while one dynasty of Turks was established in the peninsula, a second dynasty arose in the former seat of their power.

Now I call the era at which I have arrived the turning point of their fortunes, because, when they had descended down to Khorasan and the countries below it, they might have turned to the East or to the West, as they chose. They were at liberty to turn their forces eastward against their kindred in Hindostan, whom they had driven out of Ghizni and Afghanistan, or to face towards the west, and make their way thither through the Saracens of Persia and its neighboring countries. It was an era which determined the history of the world....

But this era was a turning point in their history in another and more serious respect. In Sogdiana and Khorasan, they had become converts to the Mahometan faith. You will not suppose I am going to praise a religious imposture, but no Catholic need deny that it is, considered in itself, a great improvement upon Paganism. Paganism has no rule of right and wrong, no supreme and immutable judge, no intelligible revelation, no fixed dogma whatever; on the other hand, the being of one God, the fact of His revelation, His faithfulness to His promises, the eternity of the moral law, the certainty of future retribution, were borrowed by Mahomet from the Church, and are steadfastly held by his followers. The false prophet taught much which is materially true and objectively important, whatever be its subjective and formal value and influence in the individuals who profess it. He stands in his creed between the religion of God and the religion of devils, between Christianity and idolatry, between the West and the extreme East. And so stood the Turks, on adopting his faith, at the date I am speaking of; they stood between Christ in the West, and Satan in the East, and they had to make their choice; and, alas! they were led by the circumstances of the time to oppose themselves, not to Paganism, but to Christianity. A happier lot indeed had befallen poor Sultan Mahmood than befell his kindred who followed in his wake. Mahmood, a Mahometan, went eastward and found a superstition worse than his own, and fought against it, and smote it; and the sandal doors which he tore away from the idol temple and hung up at his tomb at Gazneh, almost seemed to plead for him through centuries as the soldier and the instrument of Heaven. The tribes which followed him, Moslem also, faced westward, and found, not error but truth, and fought against it as zealously, and in doing so, were simply tools of the Evil One, and preachers of a lie, and enemies, not witnesses of God. The one destroyed idol temples, the other Christian shrines. The one has been saved the woe of persecuting the Bride of the Lamb; the other is of all races the veriest brood of the serpent which the Church has encountered since she was set up. For 800 years did the sandal gates remain at Mahmood's tomb, as a trophy over idolatry; and for 800 years have Seljuk[9] and Othman[10] been our foe.

The year 1048 of our era is fixed by chronologists as the date of the rise of the Turkish power, as far as Christendom is interested in its history[11] Sixty-three years before this date, a Turk of high rank, of the name of Seljuk, had quarreled with his native prince in Turkistan, crossed the Jaxartes with his followers, and planted himself in the territory of Sogdiana. His father had been a chief officer in the prince's court, and was the first of his family to embrace Islamism; but Seljuk, in spite of his creed, did not obtain permission to advance into Sogdiana from the Saracenic government, which at that time was in possession of the country. After several successful encounters, however, he gained admission into the city of Bokhara, and there he settled. As time went on, he fully recompensed the tardy hospitality which the Saracens had shown him; for his feud with his own country-men, whom he had left, took the shape of a religious enmity, and he fought against them as pagans and infidels, with a zeal, which was both an earnest of the devotion of his people to the faith of Mahomet, and a training for the exercise of it....

For four centuries the Turks are little or hardly heard of; then suddenly in the course of as many tens of years, and under three Sultans, they make the whole world resound with their deeds; and, while they have pushed to the East through Hindostan, in the West they have hurried down to the coasts of the Mediterranean and the Archipelago, have taken Jerusalem, and threatened Constantinople. In their long period of silence they had been sowing the seeds of future conquests; in their short period of action they were gathering the fruit of past labors and sufferings. The Saracenic empire stood apparently as before; but, as soon as a Turk showed himself at the head of a military force within its territory, he found himself surrounded by the armies of his kindred which had been so long in its pay; he was joined by the tribes of Turcomans, to whom the Romans in a former age had shown the passes of the Caucasus; and he could rely on the reserve of innumerable swarms, ever issuing out of his native desert, and following in his track. Such was the state of Western Asia in the middle of the eleventh century.

Alp Arslan, the second Sultan of the line of Seljuk, is said to signify in Turkish "the courageous lion": and the Caliph gave its possessor the Arabic appellation of Azzaddin, or "Protector of Religion." It was the distinctive work of his short reign to pass from humbling the Caliph to attacking the Greek Emperor[12]. Togrul had already invaded the Greek provinces of Asia Minor, from Cilicia to Armenia, along a line of 600 miles, and here it was that he had achieved his tremendous massacres of Christians. Alp Arslan renewed the war; he penetrated to Cæesarea in Cappadocia, attracted by the gold and pearls which incrusted the shrine of the great St. Basil. He then turned his arms against Armenia and Georgia, and conquered the hardy mountaineers of the Caucasus, who at present give such trouble to the Russians. After this he encountered, defeated, and captured the Greek Emperor. He began the battle with all the solemnity and pageantry of a hero of romance. Casting away his bow and arrows, he called for an iron mace and scimeter; he perfumed his body with musk, as if for his burial, and dressed himself in white, that he might be slain in his winding sheet. After his victory, the captive Emperor of New Rome was brought before him in a peasant's dress; he made him kiss the ground beneath his feet, and put his foot upon his neck. Then, raising him up, he struck or patted him three times with his hand, and gave him his life and, on a large ransom, his liberty.

At this time the Sultan was only forty-four years of age, and seemed to have a career of glory still before him. Twelve hundred nobles stood before his throne; two hundred thousand soldiers marched under his banner. As if dissatisfied with the South, he turned his arms against his own paternal wildernesses, with which his family, as I have related, had a feud. New tribes of Turks seem to have poured down, and were wresting Sogdiana from the race of Seljuk, as the Seljukians had wrested it from the Gaznevides. Alp had not advanced far into the country, when he met his death from the hand of a captive. A Carismian chief had withstood his progress, and, being taken, was condemned to a lingering execution. On hearing the sentence, he rushed forward upon Alp Arslan; and the Sultan, disdaining to let his generals interfere, bent his bow, but, missing his aim, received the dagger of his prisoner in his breast. His death, which followed, brings before us that grave dignity of the Turkish character, of which we have already had an example in Mahmood. Finding his end approaching, he has left on record a sort of dying confession: "In my youth," he said, "I was advised by a sage to humble myself before God, to distrust my own strength, and never to despise the most contemptible foe. I have neglected these lessons, and my neglect has been deservedly punished. Yesterday, as from an eminence, I beheld the numbers, the discipline, and the spirit of my armies; the earth seemed to tremble under my feet, and I said in my heart, Surely thou art the king of the world, the greatest and most invincible of warriors. These armies are no longer mine; and, in the confidence of my personal strength, I now fall by the hand of an assassin." On his tomb was engraven an inscription, conceived in a similar spirit. "O ye, who have seen the glory of Alp Arslan exalted to the heavens, repair to Maru, and you will behold it buried in the dust."[13] Alp Arslan was adorned with great natural qualities both of intellect and of soul. He was brave and liberal: just, patient, and sincere: constant in his prayers, diligent in his alms, and, it is added, witty in his conversation; but his gifts availed him not.

It often happens in the history of states and races, in which there is found first a rise and then a decline, that the greatest glories take place just then when the reverse is beginning or begun. Thus, for instance, in the history of the Ottoman Turks, to which I have not yet come, Soliman the Magnificent is at once the last and greatest of a series of great Sultans. So was it as regards this house of Seljuk. Malek Shah, the son of Alp Arslan, the third sovereign, in whom its glories ended, is represented to us in history in colors so bright and perfect, that it is difficult to believe we are not reading the account of some mythical personage. He came to the throne at the early age of seventeen; he was well-shaped, handsome, polished both in manners and in mind; wise and courageous, pious and sincere. He engaged himself even more in the consolidation of his empire than in its extension. He reformed abuses; he reduced the taxes; he repaired the highroads, bridges, and canals; he built an imperial mosque at Bagdad; he founded and nobly endowed a college. He patronized learning and poetry, and he reformed the calendar. He provided marts for commerce; he upheld the pure administration of justice, and protected the helpless and the innocent. He established wells and cisterns in great numbers along the road of pilgrimage to Mecca; he fed the pilgrims, and distributed immense sums among the poor. He was in every respect a great prince; he extended his conquests across Sogdiana to the very borders of China. He subdued by his lieutenants Syria and the Holy Land, and took Jerusalem. He is said to have traveled round his vast dominions twelve times. So potent was he, that he actually gave away kingdoms, and had for feudatories great princes. He gave to his cousin his territories in Asia Minor, and planted him over against Constantinople, as an earnest of future conquests; and he may be said to have finally allotted to the Turcomans the fair regions of Western Asia, over which they roam to this day.

All human greatness has its term; the more brilliant was this great

Sultan's rise, the more sudden was his extinction; and the earlier he came to his power, the earlier did he lose it. He had reigned twenty years, and was but thirty-seven years old, when he was lifted up with pride and came to his end. He disgraced and abandoned to an assassin his faithful vizir, at the age of ninety-three, who for thirty years had been the servant and benefactor of the house of Seljuk. After obtaining from the Caliph the peculiar and almost incommunicable title of "the commander of the faithful," unsatisfied still, he wished to fix his own throne in Bagdad, and to deprive his impotent superior of his few remaining honors. He demanded the hand of the daughter of the Greek Emperor, a Christian, in marriage. A few days, and he was no more; he had gone out hunting, and returned indisposed; a vein was opened, and the blood would not flow. A burning fever took him off, only eighteen days after the murder of his vizir, and less than ten before the day when the Caliph was to have been removed from Bagdad.

Such is human greatness at the best, even were it ever so innocent; but as to this poor Sultan, there is another aspect even of his glorious deeds. If I have seemed here or elsewhere in these Lectures to speak of him or his with interest or admiration, only take me, Gentlemen, as giving the external view of the Turkish history, and that as introductory to the determination of its true significance. Historians and poets may celebrate the exploits of Malek; but what were they in the sight of Him who has said that whoso shall strike against His cornerstone shall be broken; but on whomsoever it shall fall, shall be ground to powder? Looking at this Sultan's deeds as mere exhibitions of human power, they were brilliant and marvelous; but there was another judgment of them formed in the West, and other feelings than admiration roused by them in the faith and the chivalry of Christendom. Especially was there one, the divinely appointed shepherd of the poor of Christ, the anxious steward of His Church, who from his high and ancient watch tower, in the fullness of apostolic charity, surveyed narrowly what was going on at thousands of miles from him, and with prophetic eye looked into the future age; and scarcely had that enemy, who was in the event so heavily to smite the Christian world, shown himself, when he gave warning of the danger, and prepared himself with measures for averting it. Scarcely had the Turk touched the shores of the Mediterranean and the Archipelago, when the Pope detected and denounced him before all Europe. The heroic Pontiff, St. Gregory the Seventh, was then upon the throne of the Apostle; and though he was engaged in one of the severest conflicts which Pope has ever sustained, not only against the secular power, but against bad bishops and priests, yet at a time when his very life was not his own, and present responsibilities so urged him, that one would fancy he had time for no other thought, Gregory was able to turn his mind to the consideration of a contingent danger in the almost fabulous East. In a letter written during the reign of Malek Shah, he suggested the idea of a crusade against the misbeliever, which later popes carried out. He assures the Emperor of Germany, whom he was addressing, that he had 50,000 troops ready for the holy war, whom he would fain have led in person. This was in the year 1074.

In truth, the most melancholy accounts were brought to Europe of the state of things in the Holy Land. A rude Turcoman ruled in Jerusalem; his people insulted there the clergy of every profession; they dragged the patriarch by the hair along the pavement, and cast him into a dungeon, in hopes of a ransom; and disturbed from time to time the Latin Mass and office in the Church of the Resurrection. As to the pilgrims, Asia Minor, the country through which they had to travel in an age when the sea was not yet safe to the voyager, was a scene of foreign incursion and internal distraction. They arrived at Jerusalem exhausted by their sufferings, and sometimes terminated them by death, before they were permitted to kiss the Holy Sepulchre.

It is commonly said that the Crusades failed in their object; that they were nothing else but a lavish expenditure of men and treasure; and that the possession of the Holy Places by the Turks to this day is a proof of it. Now I will not enter here into a very intricate controversy; this only will I say, that, if the tribes of the desert, under the leadership of the house of Seljuk, turned their faces to the West in the middle of the eleventh century; if in forty years they had advanced from Khorasan to Jerusalem and the neighborhood of Constantinople; and if in consequence they were threatening Europe and Christianity; and if, for that reason, it was a great object to drive them back or break them to pieces; if it were a worthy object of the Crusades to rescue Europe

from this peril and to reassure the anxious minds of Christian multi-
tudes; then were the Crusades no failure in their issue, for this object
was fully accomplished. The Seljukian Turks were hurled back upon
the East, and then broken up, by the hosts of the Crusaders. The lieutenant of Malek Shah, who had been established as Sultan of Roum (as
Asia Minor was called by the Turks), was driven to an obscure town,
where his dynasty lasted, indeed, but gradually dwindled away. A
similar fate attended the house of Seljuk in other parts of the Empire,
and internal quarrels increased and perpetuated its weakness. Sudden
as was its rise, as sudden was its fall; till the terrible Zingis, descending
on the Turkish dynasties, like an avalanche, coöperated effectually
with the Crusaders and finished their work; and if Jerusalem was not
protected from other enemies, at least Constantinople was saved, and
Europe was placed in security, for three hundred years.

---

1. Ancient people living near the Oxus; called *white* from their greater degree of civilization.
2. Eastern Mahometans that crossed into Turkey, Northern Africa, and Spain. The
   Moors are a type.
3. Northeast of the river Oxus; included in modern Bokhara.
4. In Asiatic Turkey; thought to be the oldest city in the world.
5. Caliph of Bagdad; contemporaneous with Charlemagne in the eighth century.
6. Thornton.
7. The power of the European Turks, virtually broken at Lepanto, 1571, has continued
   to decline, so that were it not for the jealousy of the Powers, Turkey would long
   since have been dismembered.
8. North central province of Persia.
9. Grandfather of Togrul Beg, who founded a powerful dynasty in Central Asia.
10. Third successor of Mahomet; caliph in 644; noted for his extensive conquests and for
    having given his name to the Ottomans.
11. Baronius, Pagi.
12. Romanus Diogenes, defeated in 1071 A.D.
13. Gibbon.

THE PAST AND PRESENT OF THE OTTOMANS

I think it is clear, that, if my account be only in the main correct, the Turkish power certainly is not a civilized, and is a barbarous power. The barbarian lives without principle and without aim; he does but reflect the successive outward circumstances in which he finds himself, and he varies with them. He changes suddenly, when their change is sudden, and is as unlike what he was just before, as one fortune or external condition is unlike another. He moves when he is urged by appetite; else, he remains in sloth and inactivity. He lives, and he dies, and he has done nothing, but leaves the world as he found it. And what the individual is, such is his whole generation; and as that generation, such is the generation before and after. No generation can say what it has been doing; it has not made the state of things better or worse; for retrogression there is hardly room; for progress, no sort of material. Now I shall show that these characteristics of the barbarian are rudimental points, as I may call them, in the picture of the Turks, as drawn by those who have studied them. I shall principally avail myself of the information supplied by Mr. Thornton[1] and M. Volney[2], men of name and ability, and for various reasons preferable as authorities to writers of the present day.

"The Turks," says Mr. Thornton, who, though not blind to their shortcomings, is certainly favorable to them, "the Turks are of a grave and saturnine cast ... patient of hunger and privations, capable of enduring the hardships of war, but not much inclined to habits of industry.... They prefer apathy and indolence to active enjoyments; but when moved by a powerful stimulus they sometimes indulge in pleasures in excess." "The Turk," he says elsewhere, "stretched at his ease on the banks of the Bosphorus, glides down the stream of existence without reflection on the past, and without anxiety for the future. His life is one continued and unvaried reverie. To his imagination the whole universe appears occupied in procuring him pleasures.... Every custom invites to repose, and every object inspires an indolent voluptuousness. Their delight is to recline on soft verdure under the shade of trees, and to muse without fixing the attention, lulled by the trickling of a fountain or the murmuring of a rivulet, and inhaling through their pipe a gently inebriating vapor. Such pleasures, the highest which the rich can enjoy, are equally within the reach of the artisan or the peasant."

M. Volney corroborates this account of them: "Their behavior," he says, "is serious, austere, and melancholy; they rarely laugh, and the gayety of the French appears to them a fit of delirium. When they speak, it is with deliberation, without gestures and without passion; they listen without interrupting you; they are silent for whole days together, and they by no means pique themselves on supporting conversation. If they walk, it is always leisurely, and on business. They have no idea of our troublesome activity, and our walks backwards and forwards for amusement. Continually seated, they pass whole days smoking, with their legs crossed, their pipes in their mouths, and almost without changing their attitude." Englishmen present as great a contrast to the Ottoman as the French; as a late English traveler brings before us, apropos of seeing some Turks in quarantine: "Certainly," he says, "Englishmen are the least able to wait, and the Turks the most so, of any people I have ever seen. To impede an Englishman's locomotion on a journey, is equivalent to stopping the circulation of his blood; to disturb the repose of a Turk on his, is to reawaken him to a painful sense of the miseries of life. The one nation at rest is as much tormented as Prometheus, chained to his rock, with the vulture feeding on him; the other in motion is as uncomfortable as Ixion tied to his ever-moving wheel."[3]

However, the barbarian, when roused to action, is a very different being from the barbarian at rest. "The Turk," says Mr. Thornton, "is usually placid, hypochondriac, and unimpassioned; but, when the customary sedateness of his temper is ruffled, his passions ... are furious and uncontrollable. The individual seems possessed with all the ungovernable fury of a multitude; and all ties, all attachments, all natural and moral obligations, are forgotten or despised, till his rage subsides." A similar remark is made by a writer of the day: "The Turk on horseback has no resemblance to the Turk reclining on his carpet. He there assumes a vigor, and displays a dexterity, which few Europeans would be capable of emulating; no horsemen surpass the Turks; and, with all the indolence of which they are accused, no people are more fond of the violent exercise of riding."

So was it with their ancestors, the Tartars; now dosing on their horses or their wagons, now galloping over the plains from morning to night. However, these successive phases of Turkish character, as reported by travelers, have seemed to readers as inconsistencies in their reports; Thornton accepts the inconsistency. "The national character of the Turks," he says, "is a composition of contradictory qualities. We find them brave and pusillanimous; gentle and ferocious; resolute and inconstant; active and indolent; fastidiously abstemious, and indiscriminately indulgent. The great are alternately haughty and humble, arrogant and cringing, liberal and sordid."[4]What is this but to say in one word that we find them barbarians?

According to these distinct moods or phases of character, they will leave very various impressions of themselves on the minds of successive beholders. A traveler finds them in their ordinary state in repose and serenity; he is surprised and startled to find them so different from what he imagined; he admires and extols them, and inveighs against the prejudice which has slandered them to the European world. He finds them mild and patient, tender to the brute creation, as becomes the, children of a Tartar shepherd, kind and hospitable, self-possessed and dignified, the lowest classes sociable with each other, and the children gamesome. It is true; they are as noble as the lion of the desert, and as gentle and as playful as the fireside cat. Our traveler observes all this;[5] and seems to forget that from the humblest to the highest of the feline tribe, from the cat to the lion, the most wanton and tyrannical cruelty alternates with qualities more engaging or more elevated. Other barbarous tribes also have their innocent aspects—from the Scythians[6] in the classical poets and historians down to the Lewchoo islanders in the pages of Basil Hall.

But whatever be the natural excellences of the Turks, progressive they are not. This Sir Charles Fellows seems to allow: "My intimacy with the character of the Turks," he says, "which has led me to think so highly of their moral excellence, has not given me the same favorable impression of the development of their mental powers. Their refinement is of manners and affections; there is little cultivation or activity of mind among them." This admission implies a great deal, and brings us to a fresh consideration. Observe, they were in the eighth century of their political existence when Thornton and Volney lived among them, and these authors report of them as follows: "Their buildings," says Thornton, "are heavy in their proportions, bad in detail, both in taste and execution, fantastic in decoration, and destitute of genius. Their cities are not decorated with public monuments, whose object is to enliven or to embellish." Their religion forbids them every sort of painting, sculpture, or engraving; thus the fine arts cannot exist among them. They have no music but vocal; and know of no accompaniment except a bass of one note like that of the bagpipe. Their singing is in a great measure recitative, with little variation of note. They have scarcely any notion of medicine or surgery; and they do not allow of anatomy. As to science, the telescope, the microscope, the electric battery, are unknown, except as playthings. The compass is not universally employed in their navy, nor are its common purposes thoroughly understood. Navigation, astronomy, geography, chemistry, are either not known, or practiced only on antiquated and exploded principles. As to their civil and criminal codes of law, these are unalterably fixed in the Koran....

Compare the Rome of Junius Brutus to the Rome of Constantine, 800 years afterwards. In each of these polities there was a continuous progression, and the end was unlike the beginning; but the Turks, except that they have gained the faculty of political union, are pretty much what they were when they crossed the Jaxartes and Oxus. Again, at the time of Togrul Beg, the Greek schism[7] also took place; now from Michael Cerularius, in 1054, to Anthimus, in 1853, Patriarchs of Constantinople, eight centuries have passed of religious deadness and insensibility: a longer time has passed in China of a similar political inertness: yet China has preserved at least the civilization, and Greece the ecclesiastical science, with which they respectively passed into their long sleep; but the Turks of this day are still in the less than infancy of art, literature, philosophy, and general knowledge; and we may fairly conclude that, if they have not learned the very alphabet of science in eight hundred years, they are not likely to set to work on it in the nine hundredth.

~

It is true that in the last quarter of a century efforts have been made by the government of Constantinople to innovate on the existing condition of its people; and it has addressed itself in the first instance to certain details of daily Turkish life. We must take it for granted that it began with such changes as were easiest; if so, its failure in these small matters suggests how little ground there is for hope of success in other advances more important and difficult. Every one knows that in the details of dress, carriage, and general manners, the Turks are very different from Europeans: so different, and so consistently different, that the contrariety would seem to arise from some difference of essential principle. "This dissimilitude," says Mr. Thornton, "which pervades the whole of their habits, is so general, even in things of apparent insignificance, as almost to indicate design rather than accident...."

To learn from others, you must entertain a respect for them; no one listens to those whom he contemns. Christian nations make progress in secular matters, because they are aware they have many things to learn, and do not mind from whom they learn them, so that he be able to teach. It is true that Christianity, as well as Mahometanism, which imitated it, has its visible polity, and its universal rule, and its especial prerogatives and powers and lessons, for its disciples. But, with a Divine wisdom, and contrary to its human copyist, it has carefully guarded (if I may use the expression) against extending its revelations to any point which would blunt the keenness of human research or the activity of human toil. It has taken those matters for its field in which the human mind, left to itself, could not profitably exercise itself, or progress, if it would; it has confined its revelations to the province of theology, only indirectly touching on other departments of knowledge, so far as theological truth accidentally affects them; and it has shown an equally remarkable care in preventing the introduction of the spirit of caste or race into its constitution or administration. Pure nationalism it abhors; its authoritative documents pointedly ignore the distinction of Jew and Gentile, and warn us that the first often becomes the last; while its subsequent history has illustrated this great principle, by its awful, and absolute, and inscrutable, and irreversible passage from country to country, as its territory and its home. Such, then, it has been in the Divine counsels, and such, too, as realized in fact; but man has ways of his own, and, even before its introduction into the world, the inspired announcements, which preceded it, were distorted by the people to whom they were given, to minister to views of a very different kind. The secularized Jews, relying on the supernatural favors locally and temporally bestowed on themselves, fell into the error of supposing that a conquest of the earth was reserved for some mighty warrior of their own race, and that, in compensation of the reverses which befell them, they were to become an imperial nation.

What a contrast is presented to us by these different ideas of a universal empire! The distinctions of race are indelible; a Jew cannot become a Greek, or a Greek a Jew; birth is an event of past time; according to the Judaizers, their nation, as a nation, was ever to be dominant; and all other nations, as such, were inferior and subject. What was the necessary consequence? There is nothing men more pride themselves on than birth, for this very reason, that it is irrevocable; it can neither be given to those who have it not, nor taken away from those who have. The Almighty can do anything which admits of doing; He can compensate every evil; but a Greek poet says that there is one thing impossible to Him—to undo what is done. Without throwing the thought into a shape which borders on the profane, we may see in it the reason why the idea of national power was so dear and so dangerous to the Jew. It was his consciousness of inalienable superiority[8] that led him to regard Roman and Greek, Syrian and Egyptian, with ineffable arrogance and scorn. Christians, too, are accustomed to think of those who are not Christians as their inferiors; but the conviction which possesses them, that they have what others have not, is obviously not open to the temptation which nationalism presents. According to their own faith, there is no insuperable gulf between themselves and the rest of mankind; there is not a being in the whole world but is invited by their religion to occupy the same position as themselves, and, did he come, would stand on their very level, as if he had ever been there. Such accessions to their body they continually receive, and they are bound under obligation of duty to promote them. They never can pronounce of any one, now external to them, that he will not some day be among them; they never can pronounce of themselves that, though they are now within, they may not some day be found outside, the Divine polity. Such are the sentiments inculcated by Christianity, even in the contemplation of the very superiority which it imparts; even there it is a principle, not of repulsion between man and man, but of good fellowship; but as to subjects of secular knowledge, since here it does not arrogate any superiority at all, it has in fact no tendency whatever to center its disciple's contemplation on himself, or to alienate him from his kind. He readily acknowledges and defers to the superiority in art or science of those, if so be, who are unhappily enemies to Christianity. He admits the principle of progress on all matters of knowledge and conduct on which the Creator has not decided the truth already by revealing it; and he is at all times ready to learn, in those merely secular matters, from those who can teach him best. Thus it is that Christianity, even negatively, and without contemplating its positive influences, is the religion of civilization.

---

1. An English writer on political economy, belonging to the nineteenth century.
2. A distinguished French author. His *Travels in Egypt and Syria* is a work of high reputation.
3. Formby's Visit, p. 70.
4. Bell's Geography.
5. Vid. Sir Charles Fellows' Asia Minor.
6. In ancient times the inhabitants of all North and Northeastern Europe and Asia
7. Separation of the Greek Church from Rome. The schism was begun by the crafty, ambitious Photius in the ninth century, and consummated by Michael Cerularius in 1054.
8. A forcible proof that Christianity must be and is the religion of civilization. See Balmes on the *Civilization of Europe*.

PART III
UNIVERSITIES

WHAT IS A UNIVERSITY?

*I*f[1] I were asked to describe as briefly and popularly as I could, what a University was, I should draw my answer from its ancient designation of a *Studium Generale*, or "School of Universal Learning." This description implies the assemblage of strangers from all parts in one spot—*from all parts*; else, how will you find professors and students for every department of knowledge? and *in one spot*; else, how can there be any school at all? Accordingly, in its simple and rudimental form, it is a school of knowledge of every kind, consisting of teachers and learners from every quarter. Many things are requisite to complete and satisfy the idea embodied in this description; but such as this a University seems to be in its essence, a place for the communication and circulation of thought, by means of personal intercourse, through a wide extent of country.

Mutual education, in a large sense of the word, is one of the great and incessant occupations of human society, carried on partly with set purpose, and partly not. One generation forms another; and the existing generation is ever acting and reacting upon itself in the persons of its individual members. Now, in this process, books, I need scarcely say, that is, the *litera scripta*, are one special instrument. It is true; and emphatically so in this age. Considering the prodigious powers of the press, and how they are developed at this time in the never intermitting issue of periodicals, tracts, pamphlets, works in series, and light literature, we must allow there never was a time which promised fairer for dispensing with every other means of information and instruction. What can we want more, you will say, for the intellectual education of the whole man, and for every man, than so exuberant and diversified and persistent a promulgation of all kinds of knowledge? Why, you will ask, need we go up to knowledge, when knowledge comes down to us? The Sibyl wrote her prophecies upon the leaves of the forest, and wasted them; but here such careless profusion might be prudently indulged, for it can be afforded without loss, in consequence of the almost fabulous fecundity of the instrument which these latter ages have invented. We have sermons in stones, and books in the running brooks; works larger and more comprehensive than those which have gained for ancients an immortality, issue forth every morning, and are projected onwards to the ends of the earth at the rate of hundreds of miles a day. Our seats are strewed, our pavements are powdered, with swarms of little tracts; and the very bricks of our city walls preach wisdom, by informing us by their placards where we can at once cheaply purchase it.

I allow all this, and much more; such certainly is our popular education, and its effects are remarkable. Nevertheless, after all, even in this age, whenever men are really serious about getting what, in the language of trade, is called "a good article," when they aim at something precise, something refined, something really luminous, something really large, something choice, they go to another market; they avail themselves, in some shape or other, of the rival method, the ancient method, of oral instruction, of present communication between man and man, of teachers instead of learning, of the personal influence of a master, and the humble initiation of a disciple, and, in consequence, of great centers of pilgrimage and throng, which such a method of education necessarily involves.

If the actions of men may be taken as any test of their convictions, then we have reason for saying this, viz.: that the province and the inestimable benefit of the *litera scripta* is that of being a record of truth, and an authority of appeal, and an instrument of teaching in the hands of a teacher; but that, if we wish to become exact and fully furnished in any branch of knowledge which is diversified and complicated, we must consult the living man and listen to his living voice....

No book can convey the special spirit and delicate peculiarities of its subject with that rapidity and certainty which attend on the sympathy of mind with mind, through the eyes, the look, the accent, and the manner, in casual expressions thrown off at the moment, and the unstudied turns of familiar conversation. But I am already dwelling too long on what is but an incidental portion of my main subject. Whatever be the cause, the fact is undeniable. The general principles of any study you may learn by books at home; but the detail, the color, the tone, the air, the life which makes it live in us, you must catch all these from those in whom it lives already. You must imitate the student in French or German, who is not content with his grammar, but goes to Paris or Dresden: you must take example from the young artist, who aspires to visit the great Masters in Florence and in Rome. Till we have discovered some intellectual daguerreotype, which takes off the course of thought, and the form, lineaments, and features of truth, as completely and minutely, as the optical instrument reproduces the sensible object, we must come to the teachers of wisdom to learn wisdom, we must repair to the fountain, and drink there. Portions of it may go from thence to the ends of the earth by means of books; but the fullness is in one place alone. It is in such assemblages and congregations of intellect that books themselves, the masterpieces of human genius, are written, or at least originated.

The principle on which I have been insisting is so obvious, and instances in point are so ready, that I should think it tiresome to proceed with the subject, except that one or two illustrations may serve to explain my own language about it, which may not have done justice to the doctrine which it has been intended to enforce. For instance, the polished manners and high-bred bearing which are so difficult of attainment, and so strictly personal when attained,—which are so much admired in society, from society are acquired. All that goes to constitute a gentleman[2],—the carriage, gait, address, gestures, voice; the ease, the self-possession, the courtesy, the power of conversing, the talent of not offending; the lofty principle, the delicacy of thought, the happiness of expression, the taste and propriety, the generosity and forbearance, the candor and consideration, the openness of hand— these qualities, some of them come by nature, some of them may be found in any rank, some of them are a direct precept of Christianity; but the full assemblage of them, bound up in the unity of an individual character, do we expect they can be learned from books? are they not necessarily acquired, where they are to be found, in high society? The very nature of the case leads us to say so; you cannot fence without an antagonist, nor challenge all comers in disputation before you have supported a thesis; and in like manner, it stands to reason, you cannot learn to converse till you have the world to converse with; you cannot unlearn your natural bashfulness, or awkwardness, or stiffness, or other besetting deformity, till you serve your time in some school of manners. Well, and is it not so in matter of fact? The metropolis, the court, the great houses of the land, are the centers to which at stated times the country comes up, as to shrines of refinement and good taste; and then in due time the country goes back again home, enriched with a portion of the social accomplishments, which those very visits serve to call out and heighten in the gracious dispensers of them. We are unable to conceive how the "gentleman-like" can otherwise be maintained; and maintained in this way it is....

Religious teaching itself affords us an illustration of our subject to a certain point. It does not indeed seat itself merely in centers of the world; this is impossible from the nature of the case. It is intended for the many not the few; its subject-matter is truth necessary for us, not truth recondite and rare; but it concurs in the principle of a University so far as this, that its great instrument, or rather organ, has ever been that which nature prescribes in all education, the personal presence of a teacher, or, in theological language, Oral Tradition. It is the living voice, the breathing form, the expressive countenance, which preaches, which catechises. Truth, a subtle, invisible, manifold spirit, is poured into the mind of the scholar by his eyes and ears, through his affections, imagination, and reason; it is poured into his mind and is sealed up there in perpetuity, by propounding and repeating it, by questioning and requestioning, by correcting and explaining, by progressing and then recurring to first principles, by all those ways which are implied in the word "catechising." In the first ages, it was a work of long time; months, sometimes years, were devoted to the arduous task of disabusing the mind of the incipient Christian of its pagan errors, and of molding it upon the Christian faith. The Scriptures indeed were at hand for the study of those who could avail themselves of them; but St. Irenæus[3] does not hesitate to speak of whole races, who had been converted to Christianity, without being able to read them. To be unable to read or write was in those times no evidence of want of learning: the hermits of the deserts were, in this sense of the word, illiterate; yet the great St. Anthony, though he knew not letters, was a match in disputation for the learned philosophers who came to try him. Didymus again, the great Alexandrian theologian, was blind. The ancient discipline, called the *Disciplina Arcani*, involved the same principle. The more sacred doctrines of Revelation were not committed to books but passed on by successive tradition. The teaching on the Blessed Trinity, and the Eucharist appears to have been so handed down for some hundred years; and when at length reduced to writing, it has filled many folios, yet has not been exhausted.

But I have said more than enough in illustration; end as I began—a University is a place of concourse, whither students come from every quarter for every kind of knowledge. You cannot have the best of every kind everywhere; you must go to some great city or emporium for it. There you have all the choicest productions of nature and art all together, which you find each in its own separate place elsewhere. All the riches of the land, and of the earth, are carried up thither; there are the best markets, and there the best workmen. It is the center of trade, the supreme court of fashion, the umpire of rival talents, and the standard of things rare and precious. It is the place for seeing galleries of first-rate pictures, and for hearing wonderful voices and performers of transcendent skill. It is the place for great preachers, great orators, great nobles, great statesmen. In the nature of things, greatness and unity go together; excellence implies a center. And such, for the third or fourth time, is a University; I hope I do not weary out the reader by repeating it. It is the place to which a thousand schools make contributions; in which the intellect may safely range and speculate, sure to find its equal in some antagonist activity, and its judge in the tribunal of truth. It is a place where inquiry is pushed forward, and discoveries verified and perfected, and rashness rendered innocuous, and error exposed, by the collision of mind with mind, and knowledge with knowledge. It is the place where the professor becomes eloquent, and is a missionary and a preacher, displaying his science in its most complete and most winning form, pouring it forth with the zeal of enthusiasm, and lighting up his own love of it in the breasts of his hearers. It is the place where the catechist makes good his ground as he goes, treading in the truth day by day into the ready memory, and wedging and tightening it into the expanding reason. It is a place which wins the admiration of the young by its celebrity, kindles the affections of the middle-aged by its beauty, and rivets the fidelity of the old by its associations[4]. It is a seat of wisdom, a light of the world, a minister of the faith, an Alma Mater of the rising generation. It is this and a great deal more, and demands a somewhat better head and hand than mine to describe it well.

---

1. **Introductory Note.** Newman's purpose in these Essays is to set forth by description and statement the nature, the work, and the peculiarities of a University; the aims with which it is established, the wants it may supply, the methods it adopts, its relation to other institutions, and its general history. The illustrations of his idea of a University first appeared in the *Dublin University Gazette*; later, in one volume, *Office and Work of Universities*. In the present form the author has exchanged the title to *Historical Sketches*, but has retained the pleasantly conversational tone of the original, lest, as he says, he might become more exact and solid at the price of becoming less readable, in the judgment of a day which considers that "a great book is a great evil."
2. Dr. Newman is unconsciously painting his own portrait in this passage.
3. A Christian martyr of the second century. He was a Greek by birth, a pupil of St. Polycarp, and an eminent theologian of his day
4. Universities are both the cause and the effect of great men; and these cherish their Alma with unlimited devotion. Read Gray's *Eton*, Lowell's *Commemoration Ode*, etc., as illustrations of this point.

UNIVERSITY LIFE

ATHENS

It has been my desire, were I able, to bring before the reader what Athens may have been, viewed as what we have since called a University; and to do this, not with any purpose of writing a panegyric on a heathen city, or of denying its many deformities, or of concealing what was morally base in what was intellectually great, but just the contrary, of representing as they really were; so far, that is, as to enable him to see what a University is, in the very constitution of society and in its own idea, what is its nature and object, and what its needs of aid and support external to itself to complete that nature and to secure that object.

So now let us fancy our Scythian, or Armenian, or African, or Italian, or Gallic student, after tossing on the Saronic waves[1], which would be his more ordinary course to Athens, at last casting anchor at Piræus[2]. He is of any condition or rank of life you please, and may be made to order, from a prince to a peasant. Perhaps he is some Cleanthes, who has been a boxer in the public games. How did it ever cross his brain to betake himself to Athens in search of wisdom? or, if he came thither by accident, how did the love of it ever touch his heart? But so it was, to Athens he came with three drachms in his girdle, and he got his livelihood by drawing water, carrying loads, and the like servile occupations. He attached himself, of all philosophers, to Zeno the Stoic,—to Zeno, the most high-minded, the most haughty of speculators; and out of his daily earnings the poor scholar brought his master the daily sum of an obolus[3], in payment for attending his lectures. Such progress did he make, that on Zeno's death he actually was his successor in his school; and, if my memory does not play me false, he is the author of a hymn to the Supreme Being, which is one of the noblest effusions of the kind in classical poetry. Yet, even when he was the head of a school, he continued in his illiberal toil as if he had been a monk; and, it is said, that once, when the wind took his pallium, and blew it aside, he was discovered to have no other garment at all— something like the German student who came up to Heidelberg with nothing upon him but a great coat and a pair of pistols.

Or it is another disciple of the Porch—Stoic by nature, earlier than by profession—who is entering the city; but in what different fashion he comes! It is no other than Marcus, Emperor of Rome and philosopher. Professors long since were summoned from Athens for his service, when he was a youth, and now he comes, after his victories in the battlefield, to make his acknowledgments at the end of life, to the city of wisdom, and to submit himself to an initiation into the Eleusinian mysteries[4].

Or it is a young man of great promise as an orator, were it not for his weakness of chest, which renders it necessary that he should acquire the art of speaking without over-exertion, and should adopt a delivery sufficient for the display of his rhetorical talents on the one hand, yet merciful to his physical resources on the other. He is called Cicero; he will stop but a short time, and will pass over to Asia Minor and its cities, before he returns to continue a career which will render his name immortal; and he will like his short sojourn at Athens so well, that he will take good care to send his son thither at an earlier age than he visited it himself.

But see where comes from Alexandria (for we need not be very solicitous about anachronisms), a young man from twenty to twenty-two, who has narrowly escaped drowning on his voyage, and is to remain at Athens as many as eight or ten years, yet in the course of that time will not learn a line of Latin, thinking it enough to become accomplished in Greek composition, and in that he will succeed. He is a grave person, and difficult to make out; some say he is a Christian, something or other in the Christian line his father is for certain. His name is Gregory, he is by country a Cappadocian, and will in time become preëminently a theologian, and one of the principal Doctors of the Greek Church.

Or it is one Horace, a youth of low stature and black hair, whose father has given him an education at Rome above his rank in life, and now is sending him to finish it at Athens; he is said to have a turn for poetry: a hero he is not, and it were well if he knew it; but he is caught by the enthusiasm of the hour, and goes off campaigning with Brutus and Cassius, and will leave his shield behind him on the field of Philippi[5].

Or it is a mere boy of fifteen: his name Eunapius; though the voyage was not long, sea sickness, or confinement, or bad living on board the vessel, threw him into a fever, and, when the passengers landed in the evening at Piræus, he could not stand. His countrymen who accompanied him, took him up among them and carried him to the house of the great teacher of the day, Proæresius[6], who was a friend of the captain's, and whose fame it was which drew the enthusiastic youth to Athens. His companions understand the sort of place they are in, and, with the license of academic students, they break into the philosopher's house, though he appears to have retired for the night, and proceed to make themselves free of it, with an absence of ceremony, which is only not impudence, because Proæresius takes it so easily. Strange introduction for our stranger to a seat of learning, but not out of keeping with Athens; for what could you expect of a place where there was a mob of youths and not even the pretense of control; where the poorer lived any how, and got on as they could, and the teachers themselves had no protection from the humors and caprices of the students who filled their lecture halls? However, as to this Eunapius, Proæresius took a fancy to the boy, and told him curious stories about Athenian life. He himself had come up to the University with one Hephæstion, and they were even worse off than Cleanthes the Stoic; for they had only one cloak between them, and nothing whatever besides, except some old bedding; so when Proæresius went abroad, Hephæstion lay in bed, and practiced himself in oratory; and then Hephæstion put on the cloak, and Proæresius crept under the coverlet. At another time there was so fierce a feud between what would be called "town and gown" in an English University, that the Professors did not dare lecture in public, for fear of ill treatment.

But a freshman like Eunapius soon got experience for himself of the ways and manners prevalent in Athens. Such a one as he had hardly entered the city, when he was caught hold of by a party of the academic youth, who proceeded to practice on his awkwardness and his ignorance. At first sight one wonders at their childishness; but the like conduct obtained in the mediæval Universities; and not many months have passed away since the journals have told us of sober Englishmen, given to matter-of-fact calculations, and to the anxieties of money making, pelting each other with snowballs on their own sacred territory, and defying the magistracy, when they would interfere with their privileges of becoming boys. So I suppose we must attribute it to something or other in human nature. Meanwhile, there stands the newcomer, surrounded by a circle of his new associates, who forthwith proceed to frighten, and to banter, and to make a fool of him, to the extent of their wit. Some address him with mock politeness, others with fierceness; and so they conduct him in solemn procession across the Agora to the Baths; and as they approach, they dance about him like madmen. But this was to be the end of his trial, for the Bath was a sort of initiation; he thereupon received the pallium, or University gown, and was suffered by his tormentors to depart in peace. One alone is recorded as having been exempted from this persecution; it was a youth graver and loftier than even St. Gregory himself: but it was not from his force of character, but at the instance of Gregory, that he escaped. Gregory was his bosom friend, and was ready in Athens to shelter him when he came. It was another Saint and Doctor; the great Basil, then, (it would appear,) as Gregory, but a catechumen of the Church.

But to return to our freshman. His troubles are not at an end, though he has got his gown upon him. Where is he to lodge? whom is he to attend? He finds himself seized, before he well knows where he is, by another party of men or three or four parties at once, like foreign porters at a landing, who seize on the baggage of the perplexed stranger, and thrust half a dozen cards into his unwilling hands. Our youth is plied by the hangers-on of professor this, or sophist that, each of whom wishes the fame or the profit of having a houseful. We will say that he escapes from their hands,—but then he will have to choose for himself where he will put up; and, to tell the truth, with all the praise I have already given, and the praise I shall have to give, to the city of mind, nevertheless, between ourselves, the brick and wood which formed it, the actual tenements, where flesh and blood had to lodge (always excepting the mansions of great men of the place), do not seem to have been much better than those of Greek or Turkish towns, which are at this moment a topic of interest and ridicule in the public prints. A lively picture has lately been set before us of Gallipoli[7]. Take, says the writer,[8] a multitude of the dilapidated outhouses found in farm-yards in England, of the rickety old wooden tenements, the cracked, shutterless structures of planks and tiles, the sheds and stalls, which our bye lanes, or fish-markets, or river-sides can supply; tumble them down on the declivity of a bare bald hill; let the spaces between house and house, thus accidentally determined, be understood to form streets, winding of course for no reason, and with no meaning, up and down the town; the roadway always narrow, the breadth never uniform, the separate houses bulging or retiring below, as circumstances may have determined, and leaning forward till they meet over-head—and you have a good idea of Gallipoli. I question whether this picture would not nearly correspond to the special seat of the Muses in ancient times. Learned writers assure us distinctly that the houses of Athens were for the most part small and mean; that the streets were crooked and narrow; that the upper stories projected over the road-way; and that staircases, balustrades, and doors that opened outwards obstructed it—a remarkable coincidence of description. I do not doubt at all, though history is silent, that that roadway was jolting to carriages, and all but impassable; and that it was traversed by drains, as freely as any Turkish town now. Athens seems in these respects to have been below the average cities of its time. "A stranger," says an ancient, "might doubt, on the sudden view, if really he saw Athens."

I grant all this, and much more, if you will; but, recollect, Athens was the home of the intellectual and beautiful; not of low mechanical contrivances and material organization. Why stop within your lodgings counting the rents in your wall or the holes in your tiling, when nature and art call you away? You must put up with such a chamber, and a table, and a stool, and a sleeping board, anywhere else in the three continents; one place does not differ from another indoors; your magalia in Africa, or your grottoes in Syria are not perfection. I suppose you did not come to Athens to swarm up a ladder, or to grope about a closet: you came to see and to hear, what hear and see you could not elsewhere. What food for the intellect is it possible to procure indoors, that you stay there looking about you? do you think to read there? where are your books? do you expect to purchase books at Athens—you are much out in your calculations. True it is, we at this day, who live in the nineteenth century, have the books of Greece as a perpetual memorial; and copies there have been, since the time that they were written; but you need not go to Athens to procure them, nor would you find them in Athens. Strange to say, strange to the nineteenth century, that in the age of Plato and Thucydides, there was not, it is said, a bookshop in the whole place: nor was the book trade in existence till the very time of Augustus. Libraries, I suspect, were the bright invention of Attalus or the Ptolemies;[9] I doubt whether Athens had a library till the reign of Hadrian. It was what the student gazed on, what he heard, what he caught by the magic of sympathy, not what he read, which was the education furnished by Athens.

He leaves his narrow lodging early in the morning; and not till night, if even then, will he return. It is but a crib or kennel, in which he sleeps when the weather is inclement or the ground damp; in no respect a home. And he goes out of doors, not to read the day's newspaper, or to buy the gay shilling volume, but to imbibe the invisible atmosphere of genius, and to learn by heart the oral traditions of taste. Out he goes; and, leaving the tumble-down town behind him, he mounts the Acropolis[10] to the right, or he turns to the Areopagus[11] on the left. He goes to the Parthenon[12] to study the sculptures of Phidias; to the temple of the Dioscuri to see the paintings of Polygnotus[13]. We indeed take our Sophocles or Æschylus out of our coat pocket; but, if our sojourner at Athens would understand how a tragic poet can write, he must betake himself to the theater on the south, and see and hear the drama literally in action. Or let him go westward to the Agora[14], and there he will hear Lysias or Andocides pleading, or Demosthenes[15] haranguing. He goes farther west still, along the shade of those noble planes, which Cimon has planted there; and he looks around him at the statues and porticoes and vestibules, each by itself a work of genius and skill, enough to be the making of another city. He passes through the city gate, and then he is at the famous Ceramicus; here are the tombs of the mighty dead; and here, we will suppose, is Pericles himself, the most elevated, the most thrilling of orators, converting a funeral oration over the slain into a philosophical panegyric of the living.

Onwards he proceeds still; and now he has come to that still more celebrated Academe, which has bestowed its own name on Universities down to this day; and there he sees a sight which will be graven on his memory till he dies. Many are the beauties of the place, the groves, and the statues, and the temple, and the stream of the Cephissus flowing by; many are the lessons which will be taught him day after day by teacher or by companion; but his eye is just now arrested by one object; it is the very presence of Plato[16]. He does not hear a word that he says; he does not care to hear; he asks neither for discourse nor disputation; what he sees is a whole, complete in itself, not to be increased by addition, and greater than anything else. It will be a point in the history of his life; a stay for his memory to rest on, a burning thought in his heart, a bond of union with men of like mind, ever afterwards. Such is the spell which the living man exerts on his fellows, for good or for evil. How nature impels us to lean upon others, making virtue, or genius, or name, the qualification for our doing so! A Spaniard is said to have traveled to Italy, simply to see Livy; he had his fill of gazing, and then went back again home. Had our young stranger got nothing by his voyage but the sight of the breathing and moving Plato, had he entered no lecture room to hear, no gymnasium to converse, he had got some measure of education, and something to tell of to his grandchildren.

But Plato is not the only sage, nor the sight of him the only lesson to be learned in this wonderful suburb. It is the region and the realm of philosophy. Colleges were the inventions of many centuries later; and they imply a sort of cloistered life, or at least a life of rule, scarcely natural to an Athenian. It was the boast of the philosophic statesman of Athens, that his countrymen achieved by the mere force of nature and the love of the noble and the great, what other people aimed at by laborious discipline; and all who came among them were submitted to the same method of education. We have traced our student on his wanderings from the Acropolis to the Sacred Way; and now he is in the region of the schools. No awful arch, no window of many-colored lights marks the seats of learning there or elsewhere; philosophy lives out of doors. No close atmosphere oppresses the brain or inflames the eyelid; no long session stiffens the limbs. Epicurus[17] is reclining in his garden; Zeno looks like a divinity in his porch; the restless Aristotle[18], on the other side of the city, as if in antagonism to Plato, is walking his pupils off their legs in his Lyceum by the Ilyssus. Our student has determined on entering himself as a disciple of Theophrastus, a teacher of marvelous popularity, who has brought together two thousand pupils from all parts of the world. He himself is of Lesbos; for masters, as well as students, come hither from all regions of the earth—as befits a University. How could Athens have collected hearers in such numbers, unless she had selected teachers of such power? it was the range of territory, which the notion of a University implies, which furnished both the quantity of the one and the quality of the other. Anaxagoras was from Ionia, Carneades from Africa, Zeno from Cyprus, Protagoras from Thrace, and Gorgias from Sicily. Andromachus was a Syrian, Proæresius an Armenian, Hilarius a Bithynian, Philiscus a Thessalian, Hadrian a Syrian. Rome is celebrated for her liberality in civil matters; Athens was as liberal in intellectual. There was no narrow jealousy, directed against a Professor, because he was not an Athenian; genius and talent were the qualifications; and to bring them to Athens, was to do homage to it as a University. There was a brotherhood and a citizenship of mind.

Mind came first, and was the foundation of the academical polity; but it soon brought along with it, and gathered round itself, the gifts of fortune and the prizes of life. As time went on, wisdom was not always sentenced to the bare cloak of Cleanthes; but, beginning in rags, it ended in fine linen. The Professors became honorable and rich; and the students ranged themselves under their names, and were proud of calling themselves their countrymen. The University was divided into four great nations, as the mediæval antiquarian would style them; and in the middle of the fourth century[19], Proæresius was the leader or proctor of the Attic, Hephæstion of the Oriental, Epiphanius of the Arabic, and Diophantus of the Pontic. Thus the Professors were both patrons of clients, and hosts and *proxeni* of strangers and visitors, as well as masters of the schools: and the Cappadocian, Syrian, or Sicilian youth who came to one or other of them, would be encouraged to study by his protection, and to aspire by his example.

Even Plato, when the schools of Athens were not a hundred years old, was in circumstances to enjoy the *otium cum dignitate*. He had a villa out at Heraclea; and he left his patrimony to his school, in whose hands it remained, not only safe, but fructifying, a marvelous phenomenon in tumultuous Greece, for the long space of eight hundred years. Epicurus too had the property of the Gardens where he lectured; and these too became the property of his sect. But in Roman times the chairs of grammar, rhetoric, politics, and the four philosophies were handsomely endowed by the State; some of the Professors were themselves statesmen or high functionaries, and brought to their favorite study senatorial rank or Asiatic opulence.

Patrons such as these can compensate to the freshman, in whom we have interested ourselves, for the poorness of his lodging and the turbulence of his companions. In everything there is a better side and a worse; in every place a disreputable set and a respectable, and the one is hardly known at all to the other. Men come away from the same University at this day, with contradictory impressions and contradictory statements, according to the society they have found there; if you believe the one, nothing goes on there as it should be: if you believe the other, nothing goes on as it should *not*. Virtue, however, and decency are at least in the minority everywhere, and under some sort of a cloud or disadvantage; and this being the case, it is so much gain whenever an Herodes Atticus is found, to throw the influence of wealth and station on the side even of a decorous philosophy. A consular man, and the heir of an ample fortune, this Herod was content to devote his life to a professorship, and his fortune to the patronage of literature. He gave the sophist Ptolemo about eight thousand pounds, as the sum is calculated, for three declamations. He built at Athens a stadium six hundred feet long, entirely of white marble, and capable of admitting the whole population. His theater, erected to the memory of his wife, was made of cedar wood curiously carved. He had two villas, one at Marathon, the place of his birth, about ten miles from Athens, the other at Cephissia, at the distance of six; and thither he drew to him the *élite*, and at times the whole body of the students. Long arcades, groves of trees, clear pools for the bath, delighted and recruited the summer visitor. Never was so brilliant a lecture room as his evening banqueting hall; highly connected students from Rome mixed with the sharp-witted provincial of Greece or Asia Minor; and the flippant sciolist, and the nondescript visitor, half philosopher, half tramp, met with a reception, courteous always, but suitable to his deserts. Herod was noted for his repartees; and we have instances on record of his setting down, according to the emergency, both the one and the other.

A higher line, though a rarer one, was that allotted to the youthful

Basil. He was one of those men who seem by a sort of fascination to draw others around them even without wishing it. One might have deemed that his gravity and his reserve would have kept them at a distance; but, almost in spite of himself, he was the center of a knot of youths, who, pagans as most of them were, used Athens honestly for the purpose for which they professed to seek it; and, disappointed and displeased with the place himself, he seems nevertheless to have been the means of their profiting by its advantages. One of these was Sophronius, who afterwards held a high office in the State: Eusebius was another, at that time the bosom friend of Sophronius, and afterwards a Bishop. Celsus too is named, who afterwards was raised to the government of Cilicia by the Emperor Julian. Julian himself, in the sequel of unhappy memory, was then at Athens, and known at least to St. Gregory. Another Julian is also mentioned, who was afterwards commissioner of the land tax. Here we have a glimpse of the better kind of society among the students of Athens; and it is to the credit of the parties composing it, that such young men as Gregory and Basil, men as intimately connected with Christianity, as they were well known in the world, should hold so high a place in their esteem and love. When the two saints were departing, their companions came around them with the hope of changing their purpose. Basil persevered; but Gregory relented, and turned back to Athens for a season.

---

1. The Gulf of Ægina.
2. Commercial port of Athens.
3. A Greek coin worth about three cents. Paid by spirits to Charon for ferriage over the Styx, according to legend.
4. Secret rites of the goddess Ceres, celebrated at Eleusis.
5. Battle in which Antony defeated the conspirators that had slain Cæsar.
6. Student of Athens, a native of Armenia, famous for his gigantic stature as well as for an astounding memory, displayed in the field of rhetoric.
7. In Turkey, at the entrance to the Dardanelles. It was the first conquest of the Turks in Europe, 1354 A.D.
8. Mr. Russell's Letters in the *Times* newspaper (1854).
9. I do not go into controversy on the subject, for which the reader must have recourse to Lipsius, Morhof, Boeckh, Bekker, etc.; and this of course applies to whatever historical matter I introduce, or shall introduce.
10. The citadel of Athens, ornamented by groups of statuary immortal in beauty.
11. The chief tribunal, held on a hill named for Ares or Mars.
12. The official temple of Pallas, protectress of Athens; it is the work of Phidias, under Pericles.
13. A Greek painter, contemporaneous with Phidias. His work is in statuesque style, few colors, form and outline exquisite.

14. The commercial and political market place, located near the Acropolis. It was designed by Cimon.

15. The most famous orator of Greece, if not of all times. He learned philosophy of Plato, oratory of Isocrates. His *Philippics* are of world-wide note.

16. The Divine, on whose infant lips the bees are said to have dropped their honey. He was the pupil of Socrates and the master of Aristotle; he founded the Academy, or the Platonic School of Philosophy, and wrote the *Republic*. Plato was a man of vast intellect, high ideals, and exceptionally pure life.

17. Founder of a school of materialism whose maxim was, "Eat, drink, and be merry, for to-morrow we die." The Epicurean said, "indulge the passions," the Stoic, "crush them," the Peripatetic,—like the Christian of later times,—"control them." Imperial Athens, no less than other powers, fell when her sons ceased to follow the counsel of her wisest philosophers.—"Play the immortal."

18. Called the Stagyrite from Stagerius, his birthplace. He was preceptor to Alexander the Great and founder of the Peripatetic School, *i.e.* of scholasticism. Aristotle undoubtedly possessed the most comprehensive, keen, and logical intellect of antiquity, and his influence on the philosophical thought of all succeeding ages is incalculable. His work in the field of physical science was also profound and extensive.

19. The Golden Age of Athenian art, letters, civil and military prestige; it was the age that crowned Athens Queen of Mind.

SUPPLY AND DEMAND

THE SCHOOLMEN

$\mathscr{I}$t is most interesting to observe how the foundations of the present intellectual greatness of Europe were laid, and most wonderful to think that they were ever laid at all. Let us consider how wide and how high is the platform of our knowledge at this day, and what openings in every direction are in progress—openings of such promise, that, unless some convulsion of society takes place, even what we have attained, will in future times be nothing better than a poor beginning; and then on the other hand, let us recollect that, seven centuries ago, putting aside revealed truths, Europe had little more than that poor knowledge, partial and uncertain, and at best only practical, which is conveyed to us by the senses. Even our first principles now are beyond the most daring conjectures then; and what has been said so touchingly of Christian ideas as compared with pagan, is true in its way and degree of the progress of secular knowledge also in the seven centuries I have named.

> *"What sages would have died to learn,*
> *[Is] taught by cottage dames."*

Nor is this the only point in which the revelations of science may be compared to the supernatural revelations of Christianity. Though sacred truth was delivered once for all, and scientific discoveries are progressive, yet there is a great resemblance in the respective histories of Christianity and of Science. We are accustomed to point to the rise and spread of Christianity as a miraculous fact, and rightly so, on account of the weakness of its instruments, and the appalling weight and multiplicity of the obstacles which confronted it. To clear away those obstacles was to move mountains; yet this was done by a few poor, obscure, unbefriended men, and their poor, obscure, unbefriended followers. No social movement can come up to this marvel, which is singular and archetypical, certainly; it is a Divine work, and we soon cease to admire it in order to adore. But there is more in it than its own greatness to contemplate; it is so great as to be prolific of greatness. Those whom it has created, its children who have become such by a supernatural power, have imitated, in their own acts, the dispensation which made them what they were; and, though they have not carried out works simply miraculous, yet they have done exploits sufficient to bespeak their own unearthly origin, and the new powers which had come into the world. The revival of letters by the energy of Christian ecclesiastics and laymen, when everything had to be done, reminds us of the birth of Christianity itself, as far as a work of man can resemble a work of God.

Two characteristics, as I have already had occasion to say, are generally found to attend the history of Science: first, its instruments have an innate force, and can dispense with foreign assistance in their work; and secondly, these instruments must exist and must begin to act, before subjects are found who are to profit by their action. In plainer language, the teacher is strong, not in the patronage of great men, but in the intrinsic value and attraction of what he has to communicate; and next, he must come forward and advertise himself, before he can gain hearers. This I have expressed before, in saying that a great school of learning lived in demand and supply, and that the supply must be before the demand. Now, what is this but the very history of the preaching of the Gospel? who but the Apostles and Evangelists went out to the ends of the earth without patron, or friend, or other external advantage which could insure their success? and again, who among the multitude they enlightened would have called for their aid unless they had gone to that multitude first, and offered to it blessings which up to that moment it had not heard of? They had no commission, they had no invitation, from man; their strength lay neither in their being sent, nor in their being sent for; but in the circumstances that they had that with them, a Divine message, which they knew would at once, when it was uttered, thrill through the hearts of those to whom they spoke, and make for themselves friends in any place, strangers and outcasts as they were when they first came. They appealed to the secret wants and aspirations of human nature, to its laden conscience, its weariness, its desolateness, and its sense of the true and the Divine; nor did they long wait for listeners and disciples, when they announced the remedy of evils which were so real.

Something like this were the first stages of the process by which in mediæval Christendom the structure of our present intellectual elevation was carried forward. From Rome as from a center, as the Apostles from Jerusalem, went forth the missionaries of knowledge, passing to and fro all over Europe; and, as Metropolitan sees were the record of the presence of Apostles, so did Paris[1], Pavia, and Bologna, and Padua, and Ferrara, Pisa and Naples, Vienna, Louvain, and Oxford, rise into Universities at the voice of the theologian or the philosopher. Moreover, as the Apostles went through labors untold, by sea and land, in their charity to souls; so, if robbers, shipwrecks, bad lodging, and scanty fare are trials of zeal, such trials were encountered without hesitation by the martyrs and confessors of science. And as Evangelists had grounded their teaching upon the longing for happiness natural to man, so did these securely rest their cause on the natural thirst for knowledge: and again as the preachers of Gospel peace had often to bewail the ruin which persecution or dissension had brought upon their nourishing colonies, so also did the professors of science often find or flee the ravages of sword or pestilence in those places, which they themselves perhaps in former times had made the seats of religious, honorable, and useful learning. And lastly, as kings and nobles have fortified and advanced the interests of the Christian faith without being necessary to it, so in like manner we may enumerate with honor Charlemagne, Alfred, Henry the First of England, Joan of Navarre, and many others, as patrons of the schools of learning, without being obliged to allow that those schools could not have progressed without such countenance. These are some of the points of resemblance between the propagation of Christian truth and the revival of letters;

and, to return to the two points, to which I have particularly drawn attention, the University Professor's confidence in his own powers, and his taking the initiative in the exercise of them, I find both these distinctly recognized by Mr. Hallam in his history of Literature. As to the latter point, he says, "The schools of Charlemagne were designed to lay the basis of a learned education, *for which there was at that time no sufficient desire*"—that is, the supply was prior to the demand. As to the former: "In the twelfth century," he says, "the *impetuosity* with which men *rushed* to that source of what they deemed wisdom, the great University of Paris, *did not depend upon academical privileges or eleemosynary stipends*, though these were undoubtedly very effectual in keeping it up. The University *created patrons, and was not created by them*"—that is, demand and supply were all in all....

Bec[2], a poor monastery of Normandy, set up in the eleventh century by an illiterate soldier, who sought the cloister, soon attracted scholars to its dreary clime from Italy, and transmitted them to England. Lanfranc, afterwards Archbishop of Canterbury, was one of these, and he found the simple monks so necessitous, that he opened a school of logic to all comers, in order, says William of Malmesbury, "that he might support his needy monastery by the pay of the students." The same author adds, that "his reputation went into the most remote parts of the Latin world, and Bec became a great and famous Academy of letters." Here is an instance of a commencement without support, without scholars, in order to attract scholars, and in them to find support. William of Jumièges, too, bears witness to the effect, powerful, sudden, wide spreading, and various, of Lanfranc's advertisement of himself. The fame of Bec and Lanfranc, he says, quickly penetrated through the whole world; and "clerks, the sons of dukes, the most esteemed masters of the Latin schools, powerful laymen, high nobles, flocked to him." What words can more strikingly attest the enthusiastic character of the movement which he began, than to say that it carried away with it all classes; rich as well as poor, laymen as well as ecclesiastics, those who were in that day in the habit of despising letters, as well as those who might wish to live by them?...

---

1. The great Universities reached the zenith of excellence in the thirteenth century, the age of Pope Innocent III, St. Thomas, and Dante.

2. Famous monastery founded by a poor Norman knight, Herluin. Bec drew the great Lanfranc and others to its school. Many are accustomed to regard the Renaissance as the fountain whence have issued all streams of art, literature, and science. It is only necessary to turn to any of the teeming university or monastic centers of the twelfth and thirteenth centuries to dispel this so common illusion.

THE STRENGTH AND WEAKNESS
OF UNIVERSITIES

ABELARD

We can have few more apposite illustrations of at once the strength and weakness of what may be called the University principle, of what it can do and what it cannot, of its power to collect students, and its impotence to preserve and edify them, than the history of the celebrated Abelard[1]. His name is closely associated with the commencement of the University of Paris; and in his popularity and in his reverses, in the criticisms of John of Salisbury on his method, and the protest of St. Bernard against his teaching, we read, as in a pattern specimen, what a University professes in its essence, and what it needs for its "integrity." It is not to be supposed, that I am prepared to show this here, as fully as it might be shown; but it is a subject so pertinent to the general object of these Essays, that it may be useful to devote even a few pages to it.

The oracles of Divine Truth, as time goes on, do but repeat the one message from above which they have ever uttered, since the tongues of fire attested the coming of the Paraclete; still, as time goes on, they utter it with greater force and precision, under diverse forms, with fuller luminousness, and a richer ministration of thought statement, and argument. They meet the varying wants, and encounter the special resistance of each successive age; and, though prescient of coming errors and their remedy long before, they cautiously reserve their new enunciation of the old Truth, till it is imperatively demanded. And, as it happens in kings' cabinets, that surmises arise, and rumors spread, of what is said in council, and is in course of preparation, and secrets perhaps get wind, true in substance or in direction, though distorted in detail; so too, before the Church speaks, one or other of her forward children speaks for her, and, while he does anticipate to a certain point what she is about to say or enjoin, he states it incorrectly, makes it error instead of truth, and risks his own faith in the process. Indeed, this is actually one source, or rather concomitant, of heresy, the presence of some misshapen, huge, and grotesque foreshadow of true statements which are to come. Speaking under correction, I would apply this remark to the heresy of Tertullian[2] or of Sabellius[3], which may be considered a reaction from existing errors, and an attempt, presumptuous, and therefore unsuccessful, to meet them with those divinely appointed correctives which the Church alone can apply, and which she will actually apply, when the proper moment comes. The Gnostics boasted of their intellectual proficiency before the time of St. Irenæus, St. Athanasius, and St. Augustine; yet, when these doctors made their appearance, I suppose they were examples of that knowledge, true and deep, which the Gnostics professed. Apollinaris anticipated the work of St. Cyril and the Ephesine Council, and became a heresiarch in consequence; and, to come down to the present times, we may conceive that writers, who have impatiently fallen away from the Church, because she would not adopt their views, would have found, had they but trusted her, and waited, that she knew how to profit by them, though she never could have need to borrow her enunciations from them; for their writings contained, so to speak, truth *in the ore*, truth which they themselves had not the gift to disengage from its foreign concomitants, and safely use, which she alone could use, which she would use in her destined hour, and which became their stone of stumbling simply because she did not use it faster. Now, applying this principle to the subject before us, I observe, that, supposing Abelard to be the first master of scholastic philosophy[4], as many seem to hold, we shall have still no difficulty in condemning the author, while we honor the work. To him is only the glory of spoiling by his own self-will what would have been done well and surely under the teaching and guidance of Infallible Authority.

Nothing is more certain than that some ideas are consistent with one another, and others inconsistent; and, again, that every truth must be consistent with every other truth—hence, that all truths of whatever kind form into one large body of Truth, by virtue of the consistency between one truth and another, which is a connecting link running through them all. The science which discovers this connection is logic; and, as it discovers the connection when the truths are given, so, having one truth given and the connecting principle, it is able to go on to ascertain the other. Though all this is obvious, it was realized and acted on in the middle age with a distinctness unknown before; all subjects of knowledge were viewed as parts of one vast system, each with its own place in it, and from knowing one, another was inferred. Not indeed always rightly inferred, because the art might be less perfect than the science, the instrument than the theory and aim; but I am speaking of the principle of the scholastic method, of which Saints and Doctors were the teachers—such I conceive it to be, and Abelard was the ill-fated logician who had a principal share in bringing it into operation.

Others will consider the great St. Anselm and the school of Bec, as the proper source of Scholasticism; I am not going to discuss the question; anyhow, Abelard, and not St. Anselm, was the Professor at the University of Paris, and it is of Universities that I am speaking; anyhow, Abelard illustrates the strength and the weakness of the principle of advertising and communicating knowledge for its own sake, which I have called the University principle, whether he is, or is not, the first of scholastic philosophers or scholastic theologians. And, though I could not speak of him at all without mentioning the subject of his teaching, yet, after all, it is of him and of his teaching itself, that I am going to speak, whatever that might be which he actually taught. Since Charlemagne's time the schools of Paris had continued, with various fortunes, faithful, as far as the age admitted, to the old learning, as other schools elsewhere, when, in the eleventh century, the famous school of Bec began to develop the powers of logic in forming a new philosophy. As the inductive method rose in Bacon, so did the logical in the mediæval schoolmen; and Aristotle, the most comprehensive intellect of Antiquity, as the one who had conceived the sublime idea of mapping the whole field of knowledge, and subjecting all things to one profound analysis, became the presiding master in their lecture halls. It was at the end of the eleventh century that William of Champeaux founded the celebrated Abbey of St. Victor under the shadow of St, Geneviève, and by the dialectic methods which he introduced into his teaching, has a claim to have commenced the work of forming the University out of the Schools of Paris. For one at least, out of the two characteristics of a University, he prepared the way; for, though the schools were not public till after his day, so as to admit laymen as well as clerks, and foreigners as well as natives of the place, yet the logical principle of constructing all sciences into one system, implied of course a recognition of all the sciences that are comprehended in it. Of this William of Champeaux, or de Campellis, Abelard was the pupil; he had studied the dialectic art elsewhere, before he offered himself for his instructions; and, in the course of two years, when as yet he had only reached the age of twenty-two, he made such progress, as to be capable of quarreling with his master, and setting up a school for himself.

This school of Abelard was first situated in the royal castle of Melun; then at Corbeil, which was nearer to Paris, and where he attracted to himself a considerable number of hearers. His labors had an injurious effect upon his health; and at length he withdrew for two years to his native Britanny. Whether other causes coöperated in this withdrawal, I think, is not known; but, at the end of the two years, we find him returning to Paris, and renewing his attendance on the lectures of William, who was by this time a monk. Rhetoric was the subject of the lectures he now heard; and after a while the pupil repeated with greater force and success his former treatment of his teacher. He held a public disputation with him, got the victory, and reduced him to silence. The school of William was deserted, and its master himself became an instance of the vicissitudes incident to that gladiatorial wisdom (as I may style it) which was then eclipsing the old Benedictine method of the Seven Arts[5]. After a time, Abelard found his reputation sufficient to warrant him in setting up a school himself on Mount St. Geneviève; whence he waged incessant war against the unwearied logician, who by this time had rallied his forces to repel the young and ungrateful adventurer who had raised his hand against him. Great things are done by devotion to one idea; there is one class of geniuses, who would never be what they are, could they grasp a second. The calm philosophical mind, which contemplates parts without denying the whole, and the whole without confusing the parts, is notoriously indisposed to action; whereas single and simple views arrest the mind, and hurry it on to carry them out. Thus, men of one idea and nothing more, whatever their merit, must be to a certain extent narrow-minded; and it is not wonderful that Abelard's devotion to the new philosophy made him undervalue the Seven Arts out of which it had grown. He felt it impossible so to honor what was now to be added, as not to dishonor what existed before. He would not suffer the Arts to have their own use, since he had found a new instrument for a new purpose. So he opposed the reading of the Classics. The monks had opposed them before him; but this is little to our present purpose; it was the duty of men, who abjured the gifts of this world on the principle of mortification, to deny themselves literature just as they would deny themselves particular friendships or figured music. The doctrine which Abelard introduced and represents was founded on a different basis. He did not recognize in the poets of antiquity any other merit than that of furnishing an assemblage of elegant phrases and figures; and accordingly he asks why they should not be banished from the city of God, since Plato banished them from his own commonwealth. The *animus* of this language is clear, when we turn to the pages of John of Salisbury[6] and Peter of Blois, who were champions of the ancient learning. We find them complaining that the careful "getting up," as we now call it, "of books," was growing out of fashion. Youths once studied critically the text of poets or philosophers; they got them by heart; they analyzed their arguments; they noted down their fallacies; they were closely examined in the matters which had been brought before them in lecture; they composed. But now, another teaching was coming in; students were promised truth in a nutshell; they intended to get possession of the sum-total of philosophy in less than two or three years; and facts were apprehended, not in their substance and details, by means of living and, as it were, personal documents, but in dead abstracts and tables. Such were the reclamations to which the new Logic gave occasion.

These, however, are lesser matters; we have a graver quarrel with Abelard than that of his undervaluing the Classics. As I have said, my main object here is not what he taught, but why and how, and how he lived. Now it is certain his activity was stimulated by nothing very high, but something very earthly and sordid. I grant there is nothing morally wrong in the mere desire to rise in the world, though Ambition and it are twin sisters. I should not blame Abelard merely for wishing to distinguish himself at the University; but when he makes the ecclesiastical state the instrument of his ambition, mixes up spiritual matters with temporal, and aims at a bishopric through the medium of his logic, he joins together things incompatible, and cannot complain of being censured. It is he himself, who tells us, unless my memory plays me false, that the circumstance of William of Champeaux being promoted to the see of Chalons, was an incentive to him to pursue the same path with an eye to the same reward. Accordingly, we next hear of his attending the theological lectures of a certain master of William's, named Anselm, an old man, whose school was situated at Laon. This person had a great reputation in his day; John of Salisbury, speaking of him in the next generation, calls him the doctor of doctors; he had been attended by students from Italy and Germany; but the age had advanced since he was in his prime, and Abelard was disappointed in a teacher, who had been good enough for William. He left Anselm, and began to lecture on the prophet Ezekiel on his own resources.

Now came the time of his great popularity, which was more than his head could bear; which dizzied him, took him off his legs, and whirled him to his destruction. I spoke in my foregoing Chapter of those three qualities of true wisdom, which a University, absolutely and nakedly considered, apart from the safeguards which constitute its integrity, is sure to compromise. Wisdom[7], says the inspired writer, is *desursum*, is *pudica*, is *pacifica*, "from above, chaste, peaceable." We have already seen enough of Abelard's career to understand that his wisdom, instead of being "pacifica," was ambitious and contentious[8]. An Apostle speaks of the tongue both as a blessing and as a curse. It may be the beginning of a fire, he says, a "Universitas iniquitatis"; and alas! such did it become in the mouth of the gifted Abelard. His eloquence was wonderful; he dazzled his contemporaries, says Fulco, "by the brilliancy of his genius, the sweetness of his eloquence, the ready flow of his language, and the subtlety of his knowledge." People came to him from all quarters—from Rome, in spite of mountains and robbers; from England, in spite of the sea; from Flanders and Germany; from Normandy, and the remote districts of France; from Angers and Poitiers; from Navarre by the Pyrenees, and from Spain, besides the students of Paris itself; and among those, who sought his instructions now or afterwards, were the great luminaries of the schools in the next generation. Such were Peter of Poitiers, Peter Lombard, John of Salisbury, Arnold of Brescia, Ivo, and Geoffrey of Auxerre. It was too much for a weak head and heart, weak in spite of intellectual power; for vanity will possess the head, and worldliness the heart, of the man, however gifted, whose wisdom is not an effluence of the Eternal Light.

True wisdom is not only "pacifica," it is "pudica"; chaste as well as peaceable. Alas for Abelard! a second disgrace, deeper than ambition, is his portion now. The strong man—the Samson of the schools in the wildness of his course, the Solomon[9] in the fascination of his genius—shivers and falls before the temptation which overcame that mighty pair, the most excelling in body and in mind.

In a time when Colleges were unknown, and the young scholar was commonly thrown upon the dubious hospitality of a great city, Abelard might even be thought careful of his honor, that he went to lodge with an old ecclesiastic, had not his host's niece Eloisa lived with him. A more subtle snare was laid for him than beset the heroic champion or the all-accomplished monarch of Israel; for sensuality came upon him under the guise of intellect, and it was the high mental endowments of Eloisa, who became his pupil, speaking in her eyes, and thrilling on her tongue, which were the intoxication and the delirium of Abelard....

He is judged, he is punished; but he is not reclaimed. True wisdom is not only "pacifica," not only "pudica;" it is "desursum" too. It is a revelation from above; it knows heresy as little as it knows strife or license. But Abelard, who had run the career of earthly wisdom in two of its phases, now is destined to represent its third.

It is at the famous Abbey of St. Denis that we find him languidly rising from his dream of sin, and the suffering that followed. The bad dream is cleared away; clerks come to him, and the Abbot begging him to lecture still, for love now, as for gain before. Once more his school is thronged by the curious and the studious; but at length a rumor spreads, that Abelard is exploring the way to some novel view on the subject of the Most Holy Trinity. Wherefore is hardly clear, but about the same time the monks drive him away from the place of refuge he had gained. He betakes himself to a cell, and thither his pupils follow him. "I betook myself to a certain cell," he says, "wishing to give myself to the schools, as was my custom. Thither so great a multitude of scholars flocked, that there was neither room to house them, nor fruits of the earth to feed them," such was the enthusiasm of the student, such the attraction of the teacher, when knowledge was advertised freely, and its market opened.

Next he is in Champagne, in a delightful solitude near Nogent in the diocese of Troyes. Here the same phenomenon presents itself, which is so frequent in his history. "When the scholars knew it," he says, "they began to crowd thither from all parts; and, leaving other cities and strongholds, they were content to dwell in the wilderness. For spacious houses they framed for themselves small tabernacles, and for delicate food they put up with wild herbs. Secretly did they whisper among themselves: 'Behold, the whole world is gone out after him!' When, however, my Oratory could not hold even a moderate portion of them, then they were forced to enlarge it, and to build it up with wood and stone." He called the place his Paraclete, because it had been his consolation.

I do not know why I need follow his life further. I have said enough to illustrate the course of one, who may be called the founder, or at least the first great name, of the Parisian Schools. After the events I have mentioned he is found in Lower Britanny; then, being about forty-eight years of age, in the Abbey of St. Gildas; then with St. Geneviève again. He had to sustain the fiery eloquence of a Saint, directed against his novelties; he had to present himself before two Councils; he had to burn the book which had given offense to pious ears. His last two years were spent at Clugni on his way to Rome. The home of the weary, the hospital of the sick, the school of the erring, the tribunal of the penitent, is the city of St. Peter. He did not reach it; but he is said to have retracted what had given scandal in his writings, and to have made an edifying end. He died at the age of sixty-two, in the year of grace 1142.

In reviewing his career, the career of so great an intellect so miserably thrown away, we are reminded of the famous words of the dying scholar and jurist, which are a lesson to us all, "Heu, vitam perdidi, operosè nihil agendo."[10] A happier lot be ours!

---

1. Born in Brittany, 1079. He was a contentious, arrogant, but brilliant and fascinating rationalist. He triumphed over William of Champeaux, but was defeated in a theological contest by St. Bernard.

2. Modified Montanism; belief in rigid asceticism, the Montanists being, according to their doctrine, "Pneumatics," the Catholics, "Psychics," *i.e.* men of heaven, men of earth.

3. A heresy which attempted to *explain* the Trinity, and which denied the Personality of Jesus Christ

4. A constructive system founded by Aristotle, Christianized by Boethius, amplified by St. Anselm, Albert the Great, and others, perfected as a school, in its being harmonized with theology, by St. Thomas of Aquin. Love of subtilizing and of display, and barbarity of terminology, caused its decline after the thirteenth century. Political and religious strife also accelerated decadence, until the Council of Trent restored philosophy to its true position as queen of human sciences and handmaid of Religion. The chief feature of Christian scholastic philosophy is the harmonizing of natural and supernatural truth, *i.e.* the unifying of philosophy and theology, or the perfect conciliation of reason with faith—*distinction* without *opposition*.

5. The Trivium and Quadrivium: Grammar, Logic, Rhetoric; Music, Arithmetic, Astronomy, and Geometry,—these seven comprising the Liberal Arts.

6. Noted English scholar of the twelfth century. In disfavor with Henry II, because of his defense of St. Thomas á Becket.

7. St. James iii. 17.

8. St. James iii. 6

9. Type of bodily and of spiritual strength—strength forfeited by folly. One of Newman's striking comparisons.

10. Alas, I have wasted my life by doing nothing thoroughly.

PART IV
MISCELLANEOUS

POETRY, WITH REFERENCE TO ARISTOTLE'S POETICS

[1]

Poetry[2], according to Aristotle, is a representation of the ideal. Biography and history represent individual characters and actual facts; poetry, on the contrary, generalizing from the phenomenon of nature and life, supplies us with pictures drawn, not after an existing pattern, but after a creation of the mind. Fidelity is the primary merit of biography and history; the essence of poetry is fiction. "Poesis nihil aliud est," says Bacon, "quam historiæ imitatio ad placitum." It delineates that perfection which the imagination suggests, and to which as a limit the present system of Divine Providence actually tends. Moreover, by confining the attention to one series of events and scene of action, it bounds and finishes off the confused luxuriance of real nature; while, by a skillful adjustment of circumstances, it brings into sight the connection of cause and effect, completes the dependence of the parts one on another, and harmonizes the proportions of the whole. It is then but the type and model of history or biography, if we may be allowed the comparison, bearing some resemblance to the abstract mathematical formulæ of physics, before they are modified by the contingencies of atmosphere and friction. Hence, while it recreates the imagination by the superhuman loveliness of its views, it provides a solace for the mind broken by the disappointments and sufferings of actual life; and becomes, moreover, the utterance of the inward emotions of a right moral feeling, seeking a purity and a truth which this world will not give.

It follows that the poetical mind is one full of the eternal forms of beauty and perfection; these are its material of thought, its instrument and medium of observation; these color each object to which it directs its view. It is called imaginative, or creative, from the originality and independence of its modes of thinking, compared with the common-place and matter-of-fact conceptions of ordinary minds which are fettered down to the particular and individual. At the same time it feels a natural sympathy with everything great and splendid in the physical and moral world; and selecting such from the mass of common phenomena, incorporates them, as it were, into the substance of its own creations. From living thus in a world of its own, it speaks the language of dignity, emotion, and refinement. Figure is its neces-sary medium of communication with man; for in the feebleness of ordinary words to express its ideas, and in the absence of terms of abstract perfection, the adoption of metaphorical language is the only poor means allowed it for imparting to others its intense feelings. A metrical garb has, in all languages, been appropriated to poetry—it is but the outward development of the music and harmony within. The verse, far from being a restraint on the true poet, is the suitable index of his sense, and is adopted by his free and deliberate choice. We shall presently show the applicability of our doctrine to the various depart-ments of poetical composition; first, however, it will be right to volun-teer an explanation which may save it from much misconception and objection. Let not our notion be thought arbitrarily to limit the number of poets, generally considered such. It will be found to lower particular works, or parts of works, rather than the authors themselves; some-times to disparage only the vehicle in which the poetry is conveyed. There is an ambiguity in the word "poetry," which is taken to signify both the gift itself, and the written composition which is the result of it. Thus there is an apparent, but no real, contradiction in saying a poem may be but partially poetical; in some passages more so than in others; and sometimes not poetical at all. We only maintain, not that the writers forfeit the name of poet who fail at times to answer to our requisitions, but that they are poets only so far forth, and inasmuch as they do answer to them. We may grant, for instance, that the vulgari-ties of old Phœnix in the ninth *Iliad*[3], or of the nurse of Orestes in the

Choëphoræ[4], are in themselves unworthy of their respective authors, and refer them to the wantonness of exuberant genius; and yet maintain that the scenes in question contain much incidental poetry. Now and then the luster of the true metal catches the eye, redeeming whatever is unseemly and worthless in the rude ore; still the ore is not the metal. Nay, sometimes, and not unfrequently in Shakspeare, the introduction of unpoetical matter may be necessary for the sake of relief, or as a vivid expression of recondite conceptions, and, as it were, to make friends with the reader's imagination. This necessity, however, cannot make the additions in themselves beautiful and pleasing. Sometimes, on the other hand, while we do not deny the incidental beauty of a poem, we are ashamed and indignant on witnessing the unworthy substance in which that beauty is embedded. This remark applies strongly to the immoral compositions to which Lord Byron devoted his last years.

Now to proceed with our proposed investigation.

1. We will notice *descriptive poetry* first. Empedocles[5] wrote his physics in verse, and Oppian[6] his history of animals. Neither were poets—the one was an historian of nature, the other a sort of biographer of brutes. Yet a poet may make natural history or philosophy the material of his composition. But under his hands they are no longer a bare collection of facts or principles, but are painted with a meaning, beauty, and harmonious order not their own. Thomson has sometimes been commended for the novelty and minuteness of his remarks upon nature. This is not the praise of a poet, whose office rather is to represent known phenomena in a new connection or medium. In *L'Allegro* and *Il Penseroso* the poetical magician invests the commonest scenes of a country life with the hues, first of a cheerful, then of a pensive imagination. It is the charm of the descriptive poetry of a religious mind, that nature is viewed in a moral connection. Ordinary writers, for instance, compare aged men to trees in autumn—a gifted poet will in the fading trees discern the fading men.[7] Pastoral poetry is a description of rustics, agriculture, and cattle, softened off and corrected from the rude health of nature. Virgil, and much more Pope and others, have run into the fault of coloring too highly; instead of drawing generalized and ideal forms of shepherds, they have given us pictures of gentlemen and beaux. Their composition may be poetry, but it is not pastoral poetry.

2. The difference between poetical and historical *narrative* may be illustrated by the Tales Founded on Facts, generally of a religious character, so common in the present day, which we must not be thought to approve, because we use them for our purpose. The author finds in the circumstances of the case many particulars too trivial for public notice, or irrelevant to the main story, or partaking perhaps too much of the peculiarity of individual minds: these he omits. He finds connected events separated from each other by time or place, or a course of action distributed among a multitude of agents; he limits the scene or duration of the tale, and dispenses with his host of characters by condensing the mass of incident and action in the history of a few. He compresses long controversies into a concise argument, and exhibits characters by dialogue, and (if such be his object) brings prominently forward the course of Divine Providence by a fit disposition of his materials. Thus he selects, combines, refines, colors—in fact, poetizes. His facts are no longer actual, but ideal; a tale founded on facts is a tale generalized from facts. The authors of *Peveril of the Peak*, and of *Brambletye House*, have given us their respective descriptions of the profligate times of Charles II. Both accounts are interesting, but for different reasons. That of the latter writer has the fidelity of history; Walter Scott's picture is the hideous reality, unintentionally softened and decorated by the poetry of his own mind. Miss Edgeworth sometimes apologizes for certain incident in her tales by stating they took place "by one of those strange chances which occur in life, but seem incredible when found in writing." Such an excuse evinces a misconception of the principle of fiction, which, being the perfection of the actual, prohibits the introduction of any such anomalies of experience. It is by a similar impropriety that painters sometimes introduce unusual sunsets, or other singular phenomena of lights and forms. Yet some of Miss Edgeworth's works contain much poetry of narrative. Maneuvering is perfect in its way,—the plot and characters are natural, without being too real to be pleasing.

3. *Character* is made poetical by a like process. The writer draws indeed from experience; but unnatural peculiarities are laid aside, and harsh contrasts reconciled. If it be said the fidelity of the imitation is often its greatest merit, we have only to reply, that in such cases the pleasure is not poetical, but consists in the mere recognition. All novels and tales which introduce real characters are in the same degree unpo-

etical. Portrait painting, to be poetical, should furnish an abstract representation of an individual; the abstraction being more rigid, inasmuch as the painting is confined to one point of time. The artist should draw independently of the accidents of attitude, dress, occasional feeling, and transient action. He should depict the general spirit of his subject—as if he were copying from memory, not from a few particular sittings. An ordinary painter will delineate with rigid fidelity, and will make a caricature; but the learned artist contrives so to temper his composition, as to sink all offensive peculiarities and hardnesses of individuality, without diminishing the striking effect of the likeness, or acquainting the casual spectator with the secret of his art. Miss Edgeworth's representations of the Irish character are actual, and not poetical—nor were they intended to be so. They are interesting, because they are faithful. If there is poetry about them, it exists in the personages themselves, not in her representation of them. She is only the accurate reporter in word of what was poetical in fact. Hence, moreover, when a deed or incident is striking in itself, a judicious writer is led to describe it in the most simple and colorless terms, his own being unnecessary; for instance, if the greatness of the action itself excites the imagination, or the depth of the suffering interests the feelings. In the usual phrase, the circumstances are left "to speak for themselves."

Let it not be said that our doctrine is adverse to that individuality in the delineation of character, which is a principal charm of fiction. It is not necessary for the ideality of a composition to avoid those minuter shades of difference between man and man, which give to poetry its plausibility and life; but merely such violation of general nature, such improbabilities, wanderings, or coarseness, as interfere with the refined and delicate enjoyment of the imagination; which would have the elements of beauty extracted out of the confused multitude of ordinary actions and habits, and combined with consistency and ease. Nor does it exclude the introduction of imperfect or odious characters. The original conception of a weak or guilty mind may have its intrinsic beauty; and much more so, when it is connected with a tale which finally adjusts whatever is reprehensible in the personages themselves. Richard and Iago are subservient to the plot. Moral excellence in some characters may become even a fault. The Clytemnestra of Euripides is so interesting, that the Divine vengeance[8], which is the main subject of the drama, seems almost unjust. Lady

Macbeth, on the contrary, is the conception of one deeply learned in the poetical art. She is polluted with the most heinous crimes, and meets the fate she deserves. Yet there is nothing in the picture to offend the taste, and much to feed the imagination. Romeo and Juliet are too good for the termination to which the plot leads; so are Ophelia and the Bride of Lammermoor. In these cases there is something inconsistent with correct beauty, and therefore unpoetical. We do not say the fault could be avoided without sacrificing more than would be gained; still it is a fault. It is scarcely possible for a poet satisfactorily to connect innocence with ultimate unhappiness, when the notion of a future life is excluded. Honors paid to the memory of the dead are some alleviation of the harshness. In his use of the doctrine of a future life, Southey is admirable. Other writers are content to conduct their heroes to temporal happiness; Southey refuses present comfort to his Ladurlad, Thalaba, and Roderick, but carries them on through suffering to another world. The death of his hero is the termination of the action; yet so little in two of them, at least, does this catastrophe excite sorrowful feelings, that some readers may be startled to be reminded of the fact. If a melancholy is thrown over the conclusion of the *Roderick*, it is from the peculiarities of the hero's previous history.

4. Opinions, feelings, manners, and customs are made poetical by the delicacy or splendor with which they are expressed. This is seen in the *ode, elegy, sonnet*, and *ballad*, in which a single idea, perhaps, or familiar occurrence, is invested by the poet with pathos or dignity. The ballad of *Old Robin Gray* will serve for an instance out of a multitude; again, Lord Byron's *Hebrew Melody*, beginning, "Were my bosom as false," etc.; or Cowper's *Lines on his Mother's Picture*; or Milman's *Funeral Hymn* in the Martyr of Antioch; or Milton's *Sonnet on his Blindness*; or Bernard Barton's *Dream*. As picturesque specimens, we may name Campbell's *Battle of the Baltic*; or Joanna Baillie's *Chough and Crow*; and for the more exalted and splendid style, Gray's *Bard*; or Milton's *Hymn on the Nativity*; in which facts, with which every one is familiar, are made new by the coloring of a poetical imagination. It must all along be observed, that we are not adducing instances for their own sake; but in order to illustrate our general doctrine, and to show its applicability to those compositions which are, by universal consent, acknowledged to be poetical.

The department of poetry we are now speaking of is of much wider extent than might at first sight appear. It will include such moralizing and philosophical poems as Young's *Night Thoughts*, and Byron's *Childe Harold*. There is much bad taste, at present, in the judgment passed on compositions of this kind. It is the fault of the day to mistake mere eloquence for poetry[9]; whereas, in direct opposition to the conciseness and simplicity of the poet, the talent of the orator consists in making much of a single idea. "Sic dicet ille ut verset sæpe multis modis eandem et unam rem, ut hæreat in eâdem commoreturque sententiâ." This is the great art of Cicero himself, who, whether he is engaged in statement, argument, or raillery, never ceases till he has exhausted the subject; going round about it, and placing it in every different light, yet without repetition to offend or weary the reader. This faculty seems to consist in the power of throwing off harmonious verses, which, while they have a respectable portion of meaning, yet are especially intended to charm the ear. In popular poems, common ideas are unfolded with copiousness, and set off in polished verse— and this is called poetry. Such is the character of Campbell's *Pleasures of Hope*; it is in his minor poems that the author's poetical genius rises to its natural elevation. In *Childe Harold*, too, the writer is carried through his Spenserian stanza with the unweariness and equable fullness of accomplished eloquence; opening, illustrating, and heightening one idea, before he passes on to another. His composition is an extended funeral sermon over buried joys and pleasures. His laments over Greece, Rome, and the fallen in various engagements, have quite the character of panegyrical orations; while by the very attempt to describe the celebrated buildings and sculptures of antiquity, he seems to confess that *they* are the poetical text, his the rhetorical comment. Still it is a work of splendid talent, though, as a whole, not of the highest poetical excellence. Juvenal is perhaps the only ancient author who habitually substitutes declamation for poetry.

5. The *philosophy of mind* may equally be made subservient to poetry, as the philosophy of nature. It is a common fault to mistake a mere knowledge of the heart for poetical talent. Our greatest masters have known better—they have subjected metaphysics to their art. In Hamlet, Macbeth, Richard, and Othello, the philosophy of mind is but the material of the poet. These personages are ideal; they are effects of the contact of a given internal character with given outward circum- stances, the results of combined conditions determining (so to say) a

moral curve of original and inimitable properties. Philosophy is exhibited in the same subserviency to poetry in many parts of Crabbe's *Tales of the Hall*. In the writings of this author there is much to offend a refined taste; but, at least in the work in question, there is much of a highly poetical cast. It is a representation of the action and reaction of two minds upon each other and upon the world around them. Two brothers of different characters and fortunes, and strangers to each other, meet. Their habits of mind, the formation of those habits by external circumstances, their respective media of judgment, their points of mutual attraction and repulsion, the mental position of each in relation to a variety of trifling phenomena of everyday nature and life, are beautifully developed in a series of tales molded into a connected narrative. We are tempted to single out the fourth book, which gives an account of the childhood and education of the younger brother, and which for variety of thought as well as fidelity of description is in our judgment beyond praise. The Waverley Novels would afford us specimens of a similar excellence. One striking peculiarity of these tales is the author's practice of describing a group of characters bearing the same general features of mind, and placed in the same general circumstances; yet so contrasted with each other in minute differences of mental constitution, that each diverges from the common starting point into a path peculiar to himself. The brotherhood of villains in *Kenilworth*, of knights in *Ivanhoe*, and of enthusiasts in *Old Mortality* are instances of this. This bearing of character and plot on each other is not often found in Byron's poems. The Corsair is intended for a remarkable personage. We pass by the inconsistencies of his character, considered by itself. The grand fault is, that whether it be natural or not, we are obliged to accept the author's word for the fidelity of his portrait. We are told, not shown, what the hero was. There is nothing in the plot which results from his peculiar formation of mind. An everyday bravo might equally well have satisfied the requirements of the action. Childe Harold, again, if he is anything, is a being professedly isolated from the world, and uninfluenced by it. One might as well draw Tityrus's stags grazing in the air, as a character of this kind; which yet, with more or less alteration, passes through successive editions in his other poems. Byron had very little versatility or elasticity of genius; he did not know how to make poetry out of existing materials. He declaims in his own way, and has the upper-hand as long as he is allowed to go on; but, if interrogated on principles of nature and good sense, he is at once put out and brought to a stand.

Yet his conception of Sardanapalus and Myrrha is fine and ideal, and in the style of excellence which we have just been admiring in Shakspeare and Scott.

These illustrations of Aristotle's doctrine may suffice.

Now let us proceed to a fresh position; which, as before, shall first be broadly stated, then modified and explained. How does originality differ from the poetical talent? Without affecting the accuracy of a definition, we may call the latter the originality of right moral feeling. Originality may perhaps be defined the power of abstracting for one's self, and is in thought what strength of mind is in action. Our opinions are commonly derived from education and society. Common minds transmit as they receive, good and bad, true and false; minds of original talent feel a continual propensity to investigate subjects, and strike out views for themselves, so that even old and established truths do not escape modification and accidental change when subjected to this process of mental digestion. Even the style of original writers is stamped with the peculiarities of their minds. When originality is found apart from good sense, which more or less is frequently the case, it shows itself in paradox and rashness of sentiment, and eccentricity of outward conduct. Poetry, on the other hand, cannot be separated from its good sense, or taste, as it is called, which is one of its elements. It is originality energizing in the world of beauty; the originality of grace, purity, refinement, and good feeling. We do not hesitate to say, that poetry is ultimately founded on correct moral perception; that where there is no sound principle in exercise there will be no poetry; and that on the whole (originality being granted) in proportion to the standard of a writer's moral character will his compositions vary in poetical excellence. This position, however, requires some explanation.

Of course, then, we do not mean to imply that a poet must necessarily display virtuous and religious feeling; we are not speaking of the actual material of poetry, but of its sources. A right moral state of heart is the formal and scientific condition of a poetical mind[10]. Nor does it follow from our position that every poet must in fact be a man of consistent and practical principle; except so far as good feeling commonly produces or results from good practice. Burns was a man of inconsistent life; still, it is known, of much really sound principle at bottom. Thus his acknowledged poetical talent is in no wise inconsistent with the truth of our doctrine, which will refer the beauty which exists in his compositions to the remains of a virtuous and diviner nature within him. Nay, further than this, our theory holds good, even though it be shown that a depraved man may write a poem. As motives short of the purest lead to actions intrinsically good, so frames of mind short of virtuous will produce a partial and limited poetry. But even where this is instanced, the poetry of a vicious mind will be inconsistent and debased; that is, so far only poetry as the traces and shadows of holy truth still remain upon it. On the other hand, a right moral feeling places the mind in the very center of that circle from which all the rays have their origin and range; whereas minds otherwise placed command but a portion of the whole circuit of poetry. Allowing for human infirmity and the varieties of opinion, Milton, Spenser, Cowper, Wordsworth, and Southey may be considered, as far as their writings go, to approximate to this moral center. The following are added as further illustrations of our meaning. Walter Scott's center is chivalrous honor; Shakspeare exhibits the characteristics of an unlearned and undisciplined piety; Homer the religion of nature and conscience, at times debased by polytheism. All these poets are religious. The occasional irreligion of Virgil's poetry is painful to the admirers of his general taste and delicacy. Dryden's *Alexander's Feast* is a magnificent composition, and has high poetical beauties; but to a refined judgment there is something intrinsically unpoetical in the end to which it is devoted, the praises of revel and sensuality. It corresponds to a process of clever reasoning erected on an untrue foundation—the one is a fallacy, the other is out of taste. Lord Byron's *Manfred* is in parts intensely poetical; yet the delicate mind naturally shrinks from the spirit which here and there reveals itself, and the basis on which the drama is built. From a perusal of it we should infer, according to the above theory, that there was right and fine feeling in the poet's mind, but that the central and consistent character was wanting. From the history of his life we know this to be the fact. The connection between want of the religious principle and want of poetical feeling is seen in the instances of Hume and Gibbon, who had radically unpoetical minds. Rousseau, it may be supposed, is an exception to our doctrine. Lucretius, too, had great poetical genius; but his work evinces that his miserable philosophy was rather the result of a bewildered judgment than a corrupt heart.

According to the above theory, Revealed Religion should be especially poetical—and it is so in fact. While its disclosures have an originality in them to engage the intellect, they have a beauty to satisfy the moral nature. It presents us with those ideal forms of excellence in which a poetical mind delights, and with which all grace and harmony are associated. It brings us into a new world—a world of overpowering interest, of the sublimest views, and the tenderest and purest feelings. The peculiar grace of mind of the New Testament writers is as striking as the actual effect produced upon the hearts of those who have imbibed their spirit. At present we are not concerned with the practical, but the poetical nature of revealed truth. With Christians, a poetical view of things is a duty—we are bid to color all things with hues of faith, to see a Divine meaning in every event, and a superhuman tendency. Even our friends around are invested with unearthly brightness—no longer imperfect men, but beings taken into Divine favor, stamped with His seal, and in training for future happiness. It may be added, that the virtues peculiarly Christian are especially poetical—meekness, gentleness, compassion, contentment, modesty, not to mention the devotional virtues; whereas the ruder and more ordinary feelings are the instruments of rhetoric more justly than of poetry—anger, indignation, emulation, martial spirit, and love of independence.

---

1. **Introductory Note.** This instructive Essay on poetry forms one of the series titled *Critical and Historical Essays*. Cardinal Newman's own gifts and tastes for music and poetry render his appreciation of these arts keen, delicate, and true.
2. A profound and beautiful definition of poetry and of the poetical mind.
3. Epic of the *Fall of Troy* by Homer.
4. A tragedy by Æschylus, so named from the chorus that bear offerings to the tomb of Agamemnon.
5. A Sicilian; haughty, passionate; proclaimed himself a god; plunged into the crater of Mt. Etna.
6. A Greek poet of Cilicia; lived in the second century.
7. Thus:—
       "How quiet shows the woodland scene!
       Each flower and tree, its duty done,
       Reposing in decay serene,
       Like weary men when age is won," etc.

8. Does not the same criticism apply to Milton's Satan, a majestic spirit, punished beyond his due, and therefore worthy our admiration and pity? Compare Dante and Milton in their conception of Lucifer.
9. A finely distinguished truth, which explains why much rhetoric, even declamation, passes in our day for poetry.
10. Mark the line drawn between the sources of true poetry and the actual practices of the poet. Compare with the theory of Wordsworth, to find likenesses on this point.

THE INFINITUDE OF THE DIVINE ATTRIBUTES

1

The attributes of God, though intelligible to us on their surface,—for from our own sense of mercy and holiness and patience and consistency, we have general notions of the All-merciful and All-holy and All-patient, and of all that is proper to His Essence,—yet, for the very reason that they are infinite, transcend our comprehension, when they are dwelt upon, when they are followed out, and can only be received by faith. They are dimly shadowed out, in this very respect, by the great agents which He has created in the material world. What is so ordinary and familiar to us as the elements[2], what so simple and level to us as their presence and operation? yet how their character changes, and how they overmaster us, and triumph over us, when they come upon us in their fullness! The invisible air, how gentle is it, and intimately ours! we breathe it momentarily, nor could we live without it; it fans our cheek, and flows around us, and we move through it without effort, while it obediently recedes at every step we take, and obsequiously pursues us as we go forward. Yet let it come in its power, and that same silent fluid, which was just now the servant of our necessity or caprice, takes us up on its wings with the invisible power of an Angel, and carries us forth into the regions of space, and flings us down headlong upon the earth. Or go to the spring, and draw thence at your pleasure, for your cup or your pitcher, in supply of your wants;

you have a ready servant, a domestic ever at hand, in large quantity or in small, to satisfy your thirst, or to purify you from the dust and mire of the world. But go from home, reach the coast; and you will see that same humble element transformed before your eyes. You were equal to it in its condescension, but who shall gaze without astonishment at its vast expanse in the bosom of the ocean? who shall hear without awe the dashing of its mighty billows along the beach? who shall without terror feel it heaving under him, and swelling and mounting up, and yawning wide, till he, its very sport and mockery, is thrown to and fro, hither and thither, at the mere mercy of a power which was just now his companion and almost his slave? Or, again, approach the flame: it warms you, and it enlightens you; yet approach not too near, presume not, or it will change its nature. That very element which is so beautiful to look at, so brilliant in its character, so graceful in its figure, so soft and lambent in its motion, will be found in its essence to be of a keen, resistless nature; it tortures, it consumes, it reduces to ashes that of which it was just before the illumination and the life. So it is with the attributes of God; our knowledge of them serves us for our daily welfare; they give us light and warmth and food and guidance and succor; but go forth with Moses upon the mount and let the Lord pass by, or with Elias stand in the desert amid the wind, the earthquake, and the fire, and all is mystery and darkness; all is but a whirling of the reason, and a dazzling of the imagination, and an overwhelming of the feelings, reminding us that we are but mortal men and He is God, and that the outlines which Nature draws for us are not His perfect image, nor to be pronounced inconsistent with those further lights and depths with which it is invested by Revelation.

Say not, my brethren, that these thoughts are too austere for this season[3], when we contemplate the self-sacrificing, self-consuming charity wherewith God our Saviour has visited us. It is for that very reason that I dwell on them; the higher He is, and the more mysterious, so much the more glorious and the more subduing is the history of His humiliation. I own it, my brethren, I love to dwell on Him as the Only-begotten Word; nor is it any forgetfulness of His sacred humanity to contemplate His Eternal Person. It is the very idea, that He is God, which gives a meaning to His sufferings; what is to me a man, and nothing more, in agony, or scourged, or crucified? there are many holy martyrs, and their torments were terrible. But here I see One dropping blood, gashed by the thong, and stretched upon the Cross, and He is God. It is no tale of human woe which I am reading here; it is the record of the passion of the great Creator. The Word and Wisdom of the Father, who dwelt in His bosom in bliss ineffable from all eternity, whose very smile has shed radiance and grace over the whole creation, whose traces I see in the starry heavens and on the green earth, this glorious living God, it is He who looks at me so piteously, so tenderly from the Cross. He seems to say[4],—I cannot move, though I am omnipotent, for sin has bound Me here. I had had it in mind to come on earth among innocent creatures, more fair and lovely than them all, with a face more radiant than the Seraphim, and a form as royal as that of Archangels, to be their equal yet their God, to fill them with My grace, to receive their worship, to enjoy their company, and to prepare them for the heaven to which I destined them; but, before I carried My purpose into effect, they sinned, and lost their inheritance; and so I come indeed, but come, not in that brightness in which I went forth to create the morning stars and to fill the sons of God with melody, but in deformity and in shame, in sighs and tears, with blood upon My cheek, and with My limbs laid bare and rent. Gaze on Me, O My children, if you will, for I am helpless; gaze on your Maker, whether in contempt, or in faith and love. Here I wait, upon the Cross, the appointed time, the time of grace and mercy; here I wait till the end of the world, silent and motionless, for the conversion of the sinful and the consolation of the just; here I remain in weakness and shame, though I am so great in heaven, till the end, patiently expecting My full catalogue of souls, who, when time is at length over, shall be the reward of My passion and the triumph of My grace to all eternity.

---

1. **Introductory Note.** This and other typical addresses are comprised in *Discourses to Mixed Congregations*. The unerring taste of Newman employs the grave, dignified style suited to the subject-matter, which, however, never loses the simplicity and charm we expect in him.
2. Earth, air, fire, and water were believed primal elements by the ancients.
3. Lent, which commemorates the Sacred Passion of Christ
4. **He seems to say**: to the end. An illustration of Newman's sweet, impassioned eloquence. His sentences roll on like music of indefinable tenderness and beauty. What wonder if men "who came to scoff remained to pray," when the tones of that voice Matthew Arnold could not describe—for its singular sweetness—fell upon their listening souls?

CHRIST UPON THE WATERS

[1]

The earth is full of the marvels of Divine power; "Day to day[2] uttereth speech, and night to night showeth knowledge." The tokens of Omnipotence are all around us, in the world of matter, and the world of man; in the dispensation of nature, and in the dispensation of grace. To do impossibilities[3], I may say, is the prerogative of Him who made all things out of nothing, who foresees all events before they occur, and controls all wills without compelling them. In emblem of this His glorious attribute, He came[4] to His disciples in the passage I have read to you, walking upon the sea,—the emblem or hieroglyphic among the ancients of the impossible, to show them that what is impossible with man is possible with God. He who could walk the waters, could also ride triumphantly upon what is still more fickle, unstable, tumultuous, treacherous—the billows of human wills, human purposes, human hearts. The bark of Peter was struggling with the waves, and made no progress; Christ came to him walking upon them; He entered the boat, and by entering it He sustained it. He did not abandon Himself to it, but He brought it near to Himself; He did not merely take refuge in it, but He made Himself the strength of it, and the pledge and cause of a successful passage. "Presently," another gospel says, "the ship was at the land, whither they were going."

Such was the power of the Son of God, the Saviour of man, manifested by visible tokens in the material world, when He came upon earth; and such, too, it has ever since signally shown itself to be, in the history of that mystical ark[5] which He then formed to float upon the ocean of human opinion. He told His chosen servants to form an ark for the salvation of souls: He gave them directions how to construct it, —the length, breadth, and height, its cabins and its windows; and the world, as it gazed upon it, forthwith began to criticise. It pronounced it framed quite contrary to the scientific rules of shipbuilding; it prophesied, as it still prophesies, that such a craft was not sea-worthy; that it was not water-tight; that it would not float; that it would go to pieces and founder. And why it does not, who can say, except that the Lord is in it? Who can say why so old a framework, put together nineteen hundred years ago, should have lasted, against all human calculation, even to this day; always going, and never gone; ever failing, yet ever managing to explore new seas and foreign coasts—except that He, who once said to the rowers, "It is I, be not afraid," and to the waters, "Peace," is still in His own ark[6] which He has made, to direct and to prosper her course?

Time was, my brethren, when the forefathers of our race were a savage tribe[7], inhabiting a wild district beyond the limits of this quarter of the earth. Whatever brought them thither, they had no local attachments there or political settlement; they were a restless people, and whether urged forward by enemies or by desire of plunder, they left their place, and passing through the defiles of the mountains on the frontiers of Asia, they invaded Europe, setting out on a journey towards the farther west. Generation after generation passed away; and still this fierce and haughty race moved forward. On, on they went; but travel availed them not; the change of place could bring them no truth, or peace, or hope, or stability of heart; they could not flee from themselves. They carried with them their superstitions and their sins, their gods of iron and of clay, their savage sacrifices, their lawless witchcrafts, their hatred of their kind, and their ignorance of their destiny. At length they buried themselves in the deep forests of Germany, and gave themselves up to indolent repose; but they had not found their rest; they were still heathens, making the fair trees, the primeval work of God, and the innocent beasts of the chase, the objects and the instruments of their idolatrous worship. And, last of all, they crossed over the strait and made themselves masters of this island, and gave their very name to it; so that, whereas it had hitherto been called Britain, the southern part, which was their main seat, obtained the name of England. And now they had proceeded forward nearly as far as they could go, unless they were prepared to look across the great ocean, and anticipate the discovery of the world which lies beyond it.

What, then, was to happen to this restless race, which had sought for happiness and peace across the globe, and had not found it? Was it to grow old in its place, and dwindle away, and consume in the fever of its own heart, which admitted no remedy? or was it to become great by being overcome, and to enjoy the only real life of man, and rise to his only true dignity, by being subjected to a Master's yoke? Did its Maker and Lord see any good thing in it, of which, under His Divine nurture, profit might come to His elect, and glory to His name? He looked upon it, and He saw nothing there to claim any visitation of His grace, or to merit any relaxation of the awful penalty which its lawlessness and impiety had incurred. It was a proud race[8], which feared neither God nor man—a race ambitious, self-willed, obstinate, and hard of belief, which would dare everything, even the eternal pit, if it was challenged to do so. I say, there was nothing there of a nature to reverse the destiny which His righteous decrees have assigned to those who sin wilfully and despise Him. But the Almighty Lover of souls looked once again; and He saw in that poor, forlorn, and ruined nature, which He had in the beginning filled with grace and light, He saw in it, not what merited His favor, not what would adequately respond to His influences, not what was a necessary instrument of His purposes, but what would illustrate and preach abroad His grace, if He took pity on it. He saw in it, a natural nobleness, a simplicity, a frankness of character, a love of truth, a zeal for justice, an indignation at wrong, an admiration of purity, a reverence for law, a keen appreciation of the beautifulness and majesty of order, nay, further, a tenderness and an affectionateness of heart, which He knew would become the glorious instruments of His high will when illuminated and vivified by His supernatural gifts. And so He who, did it so please Him, could raise up children to Abraham out of the very stones of the earth, nevertheless determined in this instance in His free mercy to unite what was beautiful in nature with what was radiant in grace; and, as if those poor Anglo-Saxons had been too fair to be heathen[9], therefore did He rescue them from the devil's service and the devil's doom, and bring them into the house of His holiness and the mountain of His rest.

It is an old story and a familiar, and I need not go through it. I need not tell you, my Brethren, how suddenly the word of truth came to our ancestors in this island and subdued them to its gentle rule; how the grace of God fell on them, and, without compulsion, as the historian tells us, the multitude became Christian; how, when all was tempestuous, and hopeless, and dark, Christ like a vision of glory came walking to them on the waves of the sea. Then suddenly there was a great calm; a change came over the pagan people in that quarter of the country where the gospel was first preached to them; and from thence the blessed influence went forth, it was poured out over the whole land, till one and all, the Anglo-Saxon people, were converted by it. In a hundred years the work was done; the idols, the sacrifices, the mummeries of paganism flitted away and were not, and the pure doctrine and heavenly worship of the Cross were found in their stead. The fair form of Christianity rose up and grew and expanded like a beautiful pageant from north to south; it was majestic, it was solemn, it was bright, it was beautiful and pleasant, it was soothing to the griefs, it was indulgent to the hopes of man; it was at once a teaching and a worship; it had a dogma, a mystery, a ritual of its own; it had an hierarchical form. A brotherhood[10] of holy pastors, with miter and crosier and uplifted hand, walked forth and blessed and ruled a joyful people. The crucifix headed the procession, and simple monks were there with hearts in prayer, and sweet chants resounded, and the holy Latin tongue was heard, and boys came forth in white, swinging censers, and the fragrant cloud arose, and mass was sung, and the Saints were invoked; and day after day, and in the still night, and over the woody hills and in the quiet plains, as constantly as sun and moon and stars go forth in heaven, so regular and solemn was the stately march of blessed services on earth, high festival, and gorgeous procession, and soothing dirge, and passing bell, and the familiar evening call to prayer; till he who recollected the old pagan time, would think it all unreal that he beheld and heard, and would conclude he did but see a vision, so marvelously was heaven let down upon earth, so triumphantly were chased away the fiends of darkness to their prison below.

---

1. **Introductory Note.** This discourse was written from notes of a sermon preached at Birmingham, on occasion of the installation of Dr. Ullathorne as first bishop of the see. Again it says to us, "I believe, therefore I have spoken."
2. See Psalm xviii. 2
3. Extrinsic impossibilities, that is, those things whose elements are not metaphysically opposed, one to another.
4. See St. Matthew xiv. 24, 27
5. The Church, called the ark because prefigured by the Ark of Noe,—the House of Salvation.
6. "Behold I am with you all days, even to the consummation of the world." St. Matthew xxviii. 20.
7. The Anglo-Saxons of Teutonic stock and sprung from the Aryan branch of the human family.
8. A passage of inimitable grace and simplicity. Note the sentence-structure, the repetition of "it" in the last sentence, and other features of the consummate master.
9. On seeing some Angles in Rome, Pope Gregory exclaimed, "They should rather be called Angels than Angles."
10. Where in the range of English prose is to be found form wedded to sense in a more surpassingly beautiful way? Neither music, nor painting, nor poetry, can have anything more exquisite to yield, it would seem. *Other numbers of this volume equally admirable are The Second Spring, The Tree beside the Waters, and Intellect the Instrument of Religious Training.*

THE SECOND SPRING

Surge, propera, amica mea, columba mea, formosa mea, et veni. Jam enim hiems transiit, imber abiit et recessit. Flores apparuerunt in terrâ nostrâ.

Arise, make haste, my love, my dove, my beautiful one, and come. For the winter is now past, the rain is over and gone. The flowers have appeared in our land.

— CANT., C. II. V. 10-12

1

We have familiar experience of the order, the constancy, the perpetual renovation of the material world which surrounds us. Frail and transitory as is every part of it, restless and migratory as are its elements, never ceasing as are its changes, still it abides. It is bound together by a law of permanence, it is set up in unity; and, though it is ever dying, it is ever coming to life again. Dissolution does but give birth to fresh modes of organization, and one death is the parent of a thousand lives. Each hour, as it comes, is but a testimony, how fleeting, yet how secure, how certain, is the great whole. It is like an image on the waters, which is ever the same, though the waters ever flow. Change upon change—yet one change cries out to another, like the alternate Seraphim[2], in praise and in glory of their Maker. The sun sinks to rise again; the day is swallowed up in the gloom of the night, to be born out of it, as fresh as if it had never been quenched. Spring passes into summer, and through summer and autumn into winter, only the more surely, by its own ultimate return, to triumph over that grave, towards which it resolutely hastened from its first hour. We mourn over the blossoms of May, because they are to wither; but we know, withal, that May is one day to have its revenge upon November, by the revolution of that solemn circle which never stops—which teaches us in our height of hope, ever to be sober, and in our depth of desolation, never to despair.

And forcibly as this comes home to every one of us, not less forcible is the contrast which exists between this material world, so vigorous, so reproductive, amid all its changes, and the moral world, so feeble, so downward, so resourceless, amid all its aspirations. That which ought to come to naught, endures; that which promises a future, disappoints and is no more. The same sun shines in heaven from first to last, and the blue firmament, the everlasting mountains, reflect his rays; but where is there upon earth the champion, the hero, the law giver, the body politic, the sovereign race, which was great three hundred years ago, and is great now? Moralists and poets, often do they descant upon this innate vitality of matter, this innate perishableness of mind. Man rises to fall: he tends to dissolution from the moment he begins to be; he lives on, indeed, in his children, he lives on in his name, he lives not on in his own person. He is, as regards the manifestations of his nature here below, as a bubble that breaks, and as water poured out upon the earth. He was young, he is old, he is never young again. This is the lament over him, poured forth in verse and in prose, by Christians and by heathen. The greatest work of God's hands under the sun, he, in all the manifestations of his complex being, is born only to die. His bodily frame first begins to feel the power of this constraining law, though it is the last to succumb to it. We look at the gloom of youth with interest, yet with pity; and the more graceful and sweet it is, with pity so much the more; for, whatever be its excellence and its glory, soon it begins to be deformed and dishonored by the very force of its living on. It grows into exhaustion and collapse, till at length it crumbles into that dust out of which it was originally taken.

So is it, too, with our moral being, a far higher and diviner portion of our natural constitution; it begins with life, it ends with what is worse than the mere loss of life, with a living death. How beautiful is the human heart[3], when it puts forth its first leaves, and opens and rejoices in its spring-tide! Fair as may be the bodily form, fairer far, in its green foliage and bright blossoms, is natural virtue. It blooms in the young, like some rich flower, so delicate, so fragrant, and so dazzling. Generosity and lightness of heart and amiableness, the confiding spirit, the gentle temper, the elastic cheerfulness, the open hand, the pure affection, the noble aspiration, the heroic resolve, the romantic pursuit, the love in which self has no part,—are not these beautiful? and are they not dressed up and set forth for admiration in their best shapes, in tales and in poems? and ah! what a prospect of good is there! who could believe that it is to fade! and yet, as night follows upon day, as decrepitude follows upon health, so surely are failure, and overthrow, and annihilation, the issue of this natural virtue, if time only be allowed to it to run its course. There are those who are cut off in the first opening of this excellence, and then, if we may trust their epitaphs, they have lived like angels; but wait awhile, let them live on, let the course of life proceed, let the bright soul go through the fire and water of the world's temptations and seductions and corruptions and transformations; and, alas for the insufficiency of nature! alas for its powerlessness to persevere, its waywardness in disappointing its own promise! Wait till youth has become age; and not more different is the miniature which we have of him when a boy, when every feature spoke of hope, put side by side of the large portrait painted to his honor, when he is old, when his limbs are shrunk, his eye dim, his brow furrowed, and his hair gray, than differs the moral grace of that boyhood from the forbidding and repulsive aspect of his soul, now that he has lived to the age of man. For moroseness, and misanthropy, and selfishness, is the ordinary winter of that spring. Such is man in his own nature, and such, too, is he in his works. The noblest efforts of his genius, the conquests he has made, the doctrines he has originated, the nations he has civilized, the states he has created, they outlive himself, they outlive him by many centuries, but they tend to an end, and that end is dissolution. Powers of the world, sovereignties, dynasties, sooner or later come to nought; they have their fatal hour. The Roman conqueror[4] shed tears over Carthage, for in the destruction of the rival city he discerned too truly an augury of the fall of Rome; and at length, with the weight and the responsibilities, the crimes and the glories, of centuries upon centuries, the Imperial City fell.

Thus man and all his works are mortal; they die, and they have no power of renovation. But what is it, my Fathers, my Brothers, what is it that has happened in England just at this time? Something strange is passing over this land, by the very surprise, by the very commotion, which it excites. Were we not near enough the scene of action to be able to say what is going on,—were we the inhabitants of some sister planet possessed of a more perfect mechanism than this earth has discovered for surveying the transactions of another globe,—and did we turn our eyes thence towards England just at this season, we should be arrested by a political phenomenon as wonderful as any which the astronomer notes down from his physical field of view. It would be the occurrence of a national commotion, almost without parallel, more violent than has happened here for centuries—at least in the judgments and intentions of men, if not in act and deed. We should note it down, that soon after St. Michael's day, 1850, a storm arose in the moral world, so furious as to demand some great explanation, and to rouse in us an intense desire to gain it. We should observe it increasing from day to day, and spreading from place to place, without remission, almost without lull, up to this very hour, when perhaps it threatens worse still, or at least gives no sure prospect of alleviation. Every party in the body politic undergoes its influence,—from the Queen upon her throne, down to the little ones in the infant or day school. The ten thousands of the constituency, the sum-total of Protestant sects, the aggregate of religious societies and associations, the great body of established clergy in town and country, the bar, even the medical profession, nay, even literary and scientific circles, every class, every interest, every fireside, gives tokens of this ubiquitous storm. This would be our report of it, seeing it from the distance, and we should speculate on the cause. What is it all about? against what is it directed? what wonder has happened upon earth? what prodigious, what preternatural event is adequate to the burden of so vast an effect? We should judge rightly in our curiosity about a phenomenon like this; it must be a portentous event, and it is. It is an innovation, a miracle, I may say, in the course of human events. The physical world revolves year by year, and begins again; but the political order of things does not renew itself, does not return; it continues, but it proceeds; there is no retrogression. This is so well understood by men of the day, that with them progress is idolized as another name for good. The past never returns—it is never good; if we are to escape existing ills, it must be by going forward. The past is out of date; the past is dead. As well may the dead live to us, as well may the dead profit us, as the past return. *This*, then, is the cause of this national transport, this national cry, which encompasses us. The past *has* returned, the dead lives. Thrones are overturned, and are never restored; States live and die, and then are matter only for history. Babylon was great, and Tyre, and Egypt, and Nineveh, and shall never be great again. The English Church[5] was, and the English Church was not, and the English Church is once again. This is the portent, worthy of a cry. It is the coming in of a Second Spring[6]; it is a restoration in the moral world, such as that which yearly takes place in the physical.

Three centuries ago, and the Catholic Church, that great creation of God's power, stood in this land in pride of place. It had the honors of near a thousand years upon it; it was enthroned on some twenty sees up and down the broad country; it was based in the will of a faithful people; it energized through ten thousand instruments of power and influence; and it was ennobled by a host of Saints and Martyrs. The churches, one by one, recounted and rejoiced in the line of glorified intercessors, who were the respective objects of their grateful homage. Canterbury alone numbered perhaps some sixteen, from St. Augustine to St. Dunstan and St. Elphege, from St. Anselm and St. Thomas down to St. Edmund. York had its St. Paulinus, St. John, St. Wilfrid, and St. William; London, its St. Erconwald; Durham, its St. Cuthbert; Winton, its St. Swithun. Then there were St. Aidan of Lindisfarne, and St. Hugh of Lincoln, and St. Chad of Lichfield, and St. Thomas of Hereford, and St. Oswald and St. Wulstan of Worcester, and St. Osmund of Salisbury, and St. Birinus of Dorchester, and St. Richard of Chichester. And then, too, its religious orders, its monastic establishments, its universities, its wide relations all over Europe, its high prerogatives in the temporal state, its wealth, its dependencies, its popular honors,—where was there in the whole of Christendom a more glorious hierarchy? Mixed up with the civil institutions, with kings and nobles, with the people, found in every village and in every town,—it seemed destined to stand, so long as England stood, and to outlast, it might be, England's greatness.

But it was the high decree of heaven, that the majesty of that presence should be blotted out. It is a long story, my Fathers and Brothers —you know it well. I need not go through it. The vivifying principle of truth, the shadow of St. Peter, the grace of the Redeemer, left it. That old Church in its day became a corpse (a marvelous, an awful change!); and then it did but corrupt the air which once it refreshed, and cumber the ground[7] which once it beautified. So all seemed to be lost; and there was a struggle for a time, and then its priests were cast out or martyred. There were sacrileges innumerable. Its temples were profaned or destroyed; its revenues seized by covetous nobles, or squandered upon the ministers of a new faith. The presence of Catholicism was at length simply removed,—its grace disowned,—its power despised,—its name, except as a matter of history, at length almost unknown. It took a long time to do this thoroughly; much time, much thought, much labor, much expense; but at last it was done. Oh, that miserable day, centuries before we were born! What a martyrdom to live in it and see the fair form of Truth, moral and material, hacked piecemeal, and every limb and organ carried off, and burned in the fire, or cast into the deep! But at last the work was done. Truth was disposed of, and shoveled away, and there was a calm, a silence, a sort of peace—and such was about the state of things when we were born into this weary world.

My Fathers and Brothers, *you* have seen it on one side, and some of us on another; but one and all of us can bear witness to the fact of the utter contempt into which Catholicism had fallen by the time that we were born. You, alas, know it far better than I can know it; but it may not be out of place, if by one or two tokens, as by the strokes of a pencil, I bear witness to you from without, of what you can witness so much more truly from within. No longer the Catholic Church in the country; nay, no longer, I may say, a Catholic community; but a few adherents of the Old Religion, moving silently and sorrowfully about, as memorials of what had been. The "Roman Catholics,"—not a sect, not even an interest, as men conceived of it,—not a body, however small, representative of the Great Communion abroad,—but a mere handful of individuals, who might be counted, like the pebbles and *detritus* of the great deluge, and who, forsooth, merely happened to retain a creed which, in its day indeed, was the profession of a Church. Here a set of poor Irishmen, coming and going at harvest time, or a colony of them lodged in a miserable quarter of the vast metropolis. There, perhaps an elderly person, seen walking in the streets, grave and solitary, and strange, though noble in bearing, and said to be of good family, and a "Roman Catholic." An old-fashioned house of gloomy appearance, closed in with high walls, with an iron gate, and yews, and the report attaching to it that "Roman Catholics" lived there; but who they were, or what they did, or what was meant by calling them Roman Catholics, no one could tell—though it had an unpleasant sound, and told of form and superstition. And then, perhaps, as we went to and fro, looking with a boy's curious eyes through the great city, we might come to-day upon some Moravian chapel, or Quaker's meeting-house, and to-morrow on a chapel of the "Roman Catholics"; but nothing was to be gathered from it, except that there were lights burning there, and some boys in white, swinging censers; and what it all meant could only be learned from books, from Protestant Histories and Sermons; and they did not report well of the "Roman Catholics," but, on the contrary, deposed that they had once had power and had abused it. And then, again, we might on one occasion hear it pointedly put out by some literary man, as the result of his careful investigation, and as a recondite point of information, which few knew, that there was this difference between the Roman Catholics of England and the Roman Catholics of Ireland, that the latter had bishops, and the former were governed by four officials, called Vicars-Apostolic.

Such was about the sort of knowledge possessed of Christianity by the heathen of old time, who persecuted its adherents from the face of the earth, and then called them a *gens lucifuga*, a people who shunned the light of day. Such were Catholics in England, found in corners, and alleys, and cellars, and the housetops, or in the recesses of the country; cut off from the populous world around them, and dimly seen, as if through a mist or in twilight, as ghosts flitting to and fro, by the high Protestants, the lords of the earth. At length so feeble did they become, so utterly contemptible, that contempt gave birth to pity; and the more generous of their tyrants actually began to wish to bestow on them some favor, under the notion that their opinions were simply too absurd ever to spread again, and that they themselves, were they but raised in civil importance, would soon unlearn and be ashamed of them. And thus, out of mere kindness to us, they began to vilify our doctrines to the Protestant world, that so our very idiotcy or our secret unbelief might be our plea for mercy.

A *great* change, an *awful* contrast, between the time-honored Church of St. Augustine[8] and St. Thomas[9], and the poor remnant of their children in the beginning of the nineteenth century! It was a miracle, I might say, to have pulled down that lordly power; but there was a greater and a truer one in store. No one could have prophesied its fall, but still less would any one have ventured to prophesy its rise again. The fall was wonderful; still after all it was in the order of nature; all things come to naught: its rise again would be a different sort of wonder, for it is in the order of grace,—and who can hope for miracles, and such a miracle as this? Has the whole course of history a like to show? I must speak cautiously and according to my knowledge, but I recollect no parallel to it. Augustine, indeed, came to the same island to which the early missionaries had come already; but they came to Britons, and he to Saxons. The Arian Goths and Lombards[10], too, cast off their heresy in St. Augustine's age, and joined the Church; but they had never fallen away from her. The inspired word seems to imply the almost impossibility of such a grace as the renovation of those who have crucified to themselves again, and trodden under foot, the Son of God. Who then could have dared to hope that, out of so sacrilegious a nation as this is, a people would have been formed again unto their Saviour? What signs did it show that it was to be singled out from among the nations? Had it been prophesied some fifty years ago, would not the very notion have seemed preposterous and wild?

My Fathers, there was one of your own order, then in the maturity of his powers and his reputation. His name is the property of this diocese; yet is too great, too venerable, too dear to all Catholics, to be confined to any part of England, when it is rather a household word in the mouths of all of us. What would have been the feelings of that venerable man, the champion of God's ark in an evil time, could *he* have lived to see this day? It is almost presumptuous for one who knew him not, to draw pictures about him, and his thoughts, and his friends, some of whom are even here present; yet am I wrong in fancying that a day such as this, in which we stand, would have seemed to him a dream, or, if he prophesied of it, to his hearers nothing but a mockery? Say that one time, rapt in spirit, he had reached forward to the future, and that his mortal eye had wandered from that lowly chapel in the valley which had been for centuries in the possession of Catholics, to the neighboring height, then waste and solitary. And let him say to those about him: "

I see a bleak mount, looking upon an open country, over against that huge town, to whose inhabitants Catholicism is of so little account. I see the ground marked out, and an ample inclosure made; and plantations are rising there, clothing and circling in the space.

"And there on that high spot, far from the haunts of men, yet in the very center of the island, a large edifice, or rather pile of edifices, appears with many fronts, and courts, and long cloisters and corridors, and story upon story. And there it rises, under the invocation of the same sweet and powerful name which has been our strength and consolation in the Valley. I look more attentively at that building[11], and I see it is fashioned upon that ancient style of art which brings back the past, which had seemed to be perishing from off the face of the earth, or to be preserved only as a curiosity, or to be imitated only as a fancy. I listen, and I hear the sound of voices, grave and musical, renewing the old chant, with which Augustine greeted Ethelbert in the free air upon the Kentish strand. It comes from a long procession, and it winds along the cloisters. Priests and Religious, theologians from the schools, and canons from the Cathedral, walk in due precedence. And then there comes a vision of well-nigh twelve mitered heads; and last I see a Prince of the Church[12], in the royal dye of empire and of martyrdom, a pledge to us from Rome of Rome's unwearied love, a token that that goodly company is firm in Apostolic faith and hope. And the shadow of the Saints is there; St. Benedict[13] is there, speaking to us by the voice of bishop and of priest, and counting over the long ages through which he has prayed, and studied, and labored; there, too, is St. Dominic's white wool, which no blemish can impair, no stain can dim: and if St. Bernard be not there, it is only that his absence may make him be remembered more. And the princely patriarch, St. Ignatius, too, the St. George of the modern world, with his chivalrous lance run through his writhing foe, he, too, sheds his blessing upon that train. And others, also, his equals or his juniors in history, whose pictures are above our altars, or soon shall be, the surest proof that the Lord's arm has not waxen short, nor His mercy failed,—they, too, are looking down from their thrones on high upon the throng. And so that high company moves on into the holy place; and there, with august rite and awful sacrifice, inaugurates the great act which brings it thither." What is that act? it is the first synod of a new Hierarchy; it is the resurrection of the Church.

O my Fathers, my Brothers, had that revered Bishop so spoken then, who that had heard him but would have said that he spoke what could not be? What! those few scattered worshipers, *the* Roman Catholics, to form a Church! Shall the past be rolled back? Shall the grave open? Shall the Saxons live again to God? Shall the shepherds[14], watching their poor flocks by night, be visited by a multitude of the heavenly army, and hear how their Lord has been new-born in their own city? Yes; for grace can, where nature cannot. The world grows old, but the Church is ever young. She can, in any time, at her Lord's will, "inherit the Gentiles, and inhabit the desolate cities." "Arise, Jerusalem[15], for thy light is come, and the glory of the Lord is risen upon thee. Behold, darkness shall cover the earth, and a mist the people; but the Lord shall arise upon thee, and His glory shall be seen upon thee. Lift up thine eyes round about, and see; all these are gathered together, they come to thee; thy sons shall come from afar, and thy daughters shall rise up at thy side." "Arise, make haste, my love, my dove, my beautiful one, and come. For the winter is now past, and the rain is over and gone. The flowers have appeared in our land ... the fig tree hath put forth her green figs; the vines in flower yield their sweet smell. Arise, my love, my beautiful one, and come." It is the time for thy Visitation[16]. Arise, Mary, and go forth in thy strength into that north country, which once was thine own, and take possession of a land which knows thee not. Arise, Mother of God, and with thy thrilling voice speak to those who labor with child, and are in pain, till the babe of grace leaps within them! Shine on us, dear Lady, with thy bright countenance, like the sun in his strength, *O stella matutina*, O harbinger of peace, till our year is one perpetual May. From thy sweet eyes, from thy pure smile, from thy majestic brow, let ten thousand influences rain down, not to confound or overwhelm, but to persuade, to win over thine enemies. O Mary, my hope, O Mother undefiled, fulfill to us the promise of this Spring. A second temple rises on the ruins of the old. Canterbury has gone its way, and York is gone, and Durham is gone, and Winchester is gone. It was sore to part with them. We clung to the vision of past greatness, and would not believe it could come to naught; but the Church in England has died, and the Church lives again. Westminster and Nottingham, Beverley and Hexham, Northampton and Shrewsbury, if the world lasts, shall be names as musical to the ear, as stirring to the heart, as the glories we have lost; and Saints shall rise out of them, if God so will, and Doctors once again shall give the law to Israel, and Preachers call to penance and to justice, as at the beginning.

Yes, my Fathers and Brothers, and if it be God's blessed will, not Saints alone, not Doctors only, not Preachers only, shall be ours—but Martyrs, too, shall re-consecrate the soil to God. We know not what is before us, ere we win our own; we are engaged in a great, a joyful work, but in proportion to God's grace is the fury of His enemies. They have welcomed us as the lion greets his prey. Perhaps they may be familiarized in time with our appearance, but perhaps they may be irritated the more. To set up the Church again in England is too great an act to be done in a corner. We have had reason to expect that such a boon would not be given to us without a cross. It is not God's way that great blessings should descend without the sacrifice first of great sufferings. If the truth is to be spread to any wide extent among this people, how can we dream, how can we hope, that trial and trouble shall not accompany its going forth? And we have already, if it may be said without presumption, to commence our work withal, a large store of merits. We have no slight outfit for our opening warfare. Can we religiously suppose that the blood of our martyrs, three centuries ago and since, shall never receive its recompense? Those priests[17], secular and regular, did they suffer for no end? or rather, for an end which is not yet accomplished? The long imprisonment, the fetid dungeon, the weary suspense, the tyrannous trial, the barbarous sentence, the savage execution, the rack, the gibbet, the knife, the caldron, the numberless tortures of those holy victims, O my God, are they to have no reward? Are Thy martyrs to cry from under Thine altar for their loving vengeance on this guilty people, and to cry in vain? Shall they lose life, and not gain a better life for the children of those who perse-cuted them? Is this Thy way, O my God, righteous and true? Is it according to Thy promise, O King of Saints, if I may dare talk to Thee of justice? Did not Thou Thyself pray for Thine enemies upon the cross, and convert them? Did not Thy first Martyr[18] win Thy great Apostle, then a persecutor, by his loving prayer? And in that day of trial and desolation for England, when hearts were pierced through and through with Mary's woe, at the crucifixion of Thy body mystical, was not every tear that flowed, and every drop of blood that was shed, the seeds of a future harvest, when they who sowed in sorrow were to reap in joy?

And as that suffering of the Martyrs is not yet recompensed, so, perchance, it is not yet exhausted. Something, for what we know, remains to be undergone, to complete the necessary sacrifice. May God forbid it, for this poor nation's sake! But still could we be surprised, my Fathers and my Brothers, if the winter even now should not yet be quite over? Have we any right to take it strange, if, in this English land, the spring-time of the Church should turn out to be an English spring, an uncertain, anxious time of hope and fear, of joy and suffering,—of bright promise and budding hopes, yet withal, of keen blasts, and cold showers, and sudden storms?

One thing alone I know,—that according to our need, so will be our strength. One thing I am sure of, that the more the enemy rages against us, so much the more will the Saints in Heaven plead for us; the more fearful are our trials from the world, the more present to us will be our Mother Mary, and our good Patrons and Angel Guardians; the more malicious are the devices of men against us, the louder cry of supplication will ascend from the bosom of the whole Church to God for us. We shall not be left orphans[19]; we shall have within us the strength of the Paraclete, promised to the Church and to every member of it. My Fathers, my Brothers in the priesthood, I speak from my heart when I declare my conviction, that there is no one among you here present but, if God so willed, would readily become a martyr for His sake. I do not say you would wish it; I do not say that the natural will would not pray that that chalice might pass away; I do not speak of what you can do by any strength of yours; but in the strength of God, in the grace of the Spirit, in the armor of justice, by the consolations and peace of the Church, by the blessing of the Apostles Peter and Paul, and in the name of Christ, you would do what nature cannot do. By the intercession of the Saints on high, by the penances and good works and the prayers of the people of God on earth, you would be forcibly borne up as upon the waves of the mighty deep, and carried on out of yourselves by the fullness of grace, whether nature wished it or no. I do not mean violently, or with unseemly struggle, but calmly, gracefully, sweetly, joyously, you would mount up and ride forth to the battle, as on the rush of Angels' wings, as your fathers did before you, and gained the prize. You, who day by day offer up the Immaculate Lamb of God, you who hold in your hands the Incarnate Word under the visible tokens which He has ordained, you who again and again drain the chalice of the Great Victim[20]; who is to make you fear? what is to startle you? what to seduce you? who is to stop you, whether you are to suffer or to do, whether to lay the foundations of the Church in tears, or to put the crown upon the work in jubilation?

My Fathers, my Brothers, one word more. It may seem as if I were going out of my way in thus addressing you; but I have some sort of plea to urge in extenuation. When the English College at Rome was set up by the solicitude of a great Pontiff[21] in the beginning of England's sorrows, and missionaries were trained there for confessorship and martyrdom here, who was it that saluted the fair Saxon youths as they passed by him in the streets of the great city, with the salutation, "Salvete flores martyrum"? And when the time came for each in turn to leave that peaceful home, and to go forth to the conflict, to whom did they betake themselves before leaving Rome, to receive a blessing which might nerve them for their work? They went for a Saint's blessing; they went to a calm old man, who had never seen blood, except in penance; who had longed indeed to die for Christ, what time the great St. Francis[22] opened the way to the far East, but who had been fixed as if a sentinel in the holy city, and walked up and down for fifty years on one beat, while his brethren were in the battle. Oh! the fire of that heart, too great for its frail tenement, which tormented him to be kept at home when the whole Church was at war! and therefore came those bright-haired strangers to him, ere they set out for the scene of their passion, that the full zeal and love pent up in that burning breast might find a vent, and flow over, from him who was kept at home, upon those who were to face the foe. Therefore one by one, each in his turn, those youthful soldiers came to the old man; and one by one they persevered and gained the crown and the palm,—all but one, who had not gone, and would not go, for the salutary blessing.

My Fathers, my Brothers, that old man was my own St. Philip[23]. Bear with me for his sake. If I have spoken too seriously, his sweet smile shall temper it. As he was with you three centuries ago in Rome, when our Temple fell, so now surely when it is rising, it is a pleasant token that he should have even set out on his travels to you; and that, as if remembering how he interceded for you at home, and recognizing the relations he then formed with you, he should now be wishing to have a name among you, and to be loved by you, and perchance to do you a service, here in your own land.

---

1. **Introductory Note.** This discourse was given in St. Mary's, Oscott, on the restoration of the Catholic hierarchy to England. It furnishes an excellent specimen of the simplicity and grace of Newman's style. The climax is reached in the glory of the last pages.
2. The angelic choirs whom St. John in vision heard crying, "Holy, Holy, Holy, Lord God Almighty." Apocalypse iv. 8.
3. A strong presentation of the weakness of human nature left to itself. "Without me you can do nothing," says Christ. John xv. 5.
4. Scipio Africanus, victor of the Carthaginians in the Third Punic War.
5. The Catholic Church in England was virtually destroyed by Henry VIII, restored by Mary I, and officially re-destroyed by Elizabeth, who attempted, through Matthew Parker, to create new orders. The Second Spring is the resuscitation of the Church in England, 1850.
6. 1515-1595. An Italian saint, contemporaneous with St. Ignatius of Loyola, who established the Society of Jesus. St. Philip Neri founded the Oratorians, a body devoted to preaching and to education.
7. "Why doth it (the barren fig tree) cumber the ground?" Newman's writings, like St. Augustine's, are saturated with Scripture.
8. Called St. Austin, sent by Gregory the Great to convert the Anglo-Saxons, 597 A.D.
9. Martyred at Canterbury by the nobles of Henry II because of his fearless defense of the rights of the Church. The Pilgrims in Chaucer's *Canterbury Tales* are on their way to the shrine of St. Thomas á Becket.
10. Barbarians that successively conquered and occupied Italy; from the fifth to the eighth century their power was felt. They embraced the heresy of Arius instead of true Christianity.
11. Cathedral of Westminster, built in Gothic style.
12. Cardinal Archbishop Wiseman, clad in purple as bishop; in red, as cardinal. In his person the hierarchy was restored to England.
13. Founder of monasticism in the West. Europe owes much of its progress in early centuries to the zeal and intelligence of the Benedictine monks,—builders of churches and schools, makers of laws, tillers of lands.
14. They who heard from angels the tidings of Christ's birth in Bethlehem.
15. Quotations from *Isaias* and the *Canticle of Canticles*.
16. Allusion to Mary's going over the hill country to visit her cousin Elisabeth. At the presence of Mary, the unborn child of Elisabeth, John the Baptist, leaped for joy and was sanctified by the grace of Christ.
17. The first are those bound by vows to observe a religious rule, as the Dominicans; the second are those under obedience to their bishop, and bound only by the vow of celibacy.
18. St. Stephen, whose death won the conversion of St. Paul. Note the beauty of the apostrophe.
19. "I will not leave you orphans." John xiv. 18.
20. Reference to the august Sacrifice of the Mass.

21. Gregory XIII, 1572-1585, established colleges for the spread of the Faith; his work was continued by Gregory XV in the Propaganda; but it was left for Pope Urban VIII to create the great missionary colleges for the six nations.
22. Xavier, the illustrious Jesuit, who converted millions to Christ in India and Japan; he died on his way to China, in the latter part of the sixteenth century.
23. 1515-1595. An Italian saint, contemporaneous with St. Ignatius of Loyola, who established the Society of Jesus. St. Philip Neri founded the Oratorians, a body devoted to preaching and to education.

ST. PAUL'S CHARACTERISTIC GIFT

Libenter igitur gloriabor in infirmitatibus meis, ut inhabitet in me virtus Christi.

Gladly therefore will I glory in my infirmities, that the power of Christ may dwell in me.

— EP. II. S. PAUL AD COR., C. XII. V. 9

1

All the Saints, from the beginning of history to the end, resemble each other in this, that their excellence is supernatural, their deeds heroic, their merits extraordinary and prevailing. They all are choice patterns of the theological virtues[2]; they all are blessed with a rare and special union with their Maker and Lord; they all lead lives of penance; and when they leave this world, they are spared that torment, which the multitude of holy souls are allotted, between earth and heaven, death and eternal glory. But, with all these various tokens of their belonging to one and the same celestial family, they may still be divided, in their external aspect, into two classes. There are those, on the one hand, who are so absorbed in the Divine life, that they seem, even while they are in the flesh, to have no part in earth or in human nature; but to think, speak, and act under views, affections, and motives simply supernatural. If they love others, it is simply because they love God, and because man is the object either of His compassion, or of His praise. If they rejoice, it is in what is unseen; if they feel interest, it is in what is unearthly; if they speak, it is almost with the voice of Angels; if they eat or drink, it is almost of Angels' food alone—for it is recorded in their histories, that for weeks they have fed on nothing else but that Heavenly Bread[3] which is the proper sustenance of the soul. Such we may suppose to have been St. John; such St. Mary Magdalen; such the hermits of the desert; such many of the holy Virgins whose lives belong to the science of mystical theology.

On the other hand, there are those, and of the highest order of sanctity too, as far as our eyes can see, in whom the supernatural combines with nature, instead of superseding it,—invigorating it, elevating it, ennobling it; and who are not the less men, because they are saints. They do not put away their natural endowments, but use them to the glory of the Giver; they do not act beside them, but through them; they do not eclipse them by the brightness of Divine grace, but only transfigure them. They are versed in human knowledge; they are busy in human society; they understand the human heart; they can throw themselves into the minds of other men; and all this in consequence of natural gifts and secular education. While they themselves stand secure in the blessedness of purity and peace, they can follow in imagination the ten thousand aberrations of pride, passion, and remorse. The world is to them a book, to which they are drawn for its own sake, which they read fluently, which interests them naturally,—though, by the reason of the grace which dwells within them, they study it and hold converse with it for the glory of God and the salvation of souls. Thus they have the thoughts, feelings, frames of mind, attractions, sympathies, antipathies of other men, so far as these are not sinful, only they have these properties of human nature purified, sanctified, and exalted; and they are only made more eloquent, more poetical, more profound, more intellectual, by reason of their being more holy. In this latter class I may perhaps without presumption place many of the early Fathers, St. Chrysostom, St. Gregory Nazianzen, St. Athanasius, and above all, the great Saint of this day, St. Paul the Apostle.

I think it a happy circumstance that, in this Church, placed, as it is, under the patronage of the great names of St. Peter and St. Paul, the special feast days of these two Apostles (for such we may account the 29th of June as regards St. Peter, and to-day as regards St. Paul) should, in the first year of our assembling here, each have fallen on a Sunday. And now that we have arrived, through God's protecting Providence, at the latter of these two days, the Conversion of St. Paul[4], I do not like to forego the opportunity, with whatever misgivings as to my ability, of offering to you, my brethren, at least a few remarks upon the wonderful work of God's creative grace mercifully presented to our inspection in the person of this great Apostle. Most unworthy of him, I know, is the best that I can say; and even that best I cannot duly exhibit in the space of time allowed me on an occasion such as this; but what is said out of devotion to him, and for the Divine glory, will, I trust, have its use, defective though it be, and be a plea for his favorable notice of those who say it, and be graciously accepted by his and our Lord and Master. Now, since I have begun by contrasting St. Paul with St. John, and by implying that St. John lived a life more simply super-natural than St. Paul, I may seem to you, my brethren, to be speaking to St. Paul's disparagement; and you may therefore ask me whether it is possible for any Saint on earth to have a more intimate communion with the Divine Majesty than was granted to St. Paul. You may remind me of his own words, "I live, now not I, but Christ liveth in me; and, that I now live in the flesh, I live in the faith of the Son of God, who loved me, and delivered Himself for me." And you may refer to his most astonishing ecstasies and visions; as when he was rapt even to the third heaven, and heard sacred words, which it "is not granted to man to utter." You may say, he "no way came short" of St. John in his awful initiation into the mysteries of the kingdom of heaven. Certainly you may say so; nor am I imagining anything contrary to you. We indeed cannot compare Saints; but I agree with you, that St. Paul was visited by favors, equal, in our apprehensions, to those which were granted to St. John. But then, on the other hand, neither was St. John behind St. Paul in these tokens of Divine love. In truth, these tokens are some of those very things which, in a greater or less degree, belong to all Saints whatever, as I said when I began; whereas my question just now is, not what are those points in which St. Paul agrees with all other Saints, but what is his distinguished mark, how we recognize him from others, what there is special in him; and I think his character-istic is this,—that, as I have said, in him the fullness of Divine gifts does not tend to destroy what is human in him, but to spiritualize and perfect it. According to his own words, used on another subject, but laying down, as it were, the principle on which his own character was formed,—"We would not be *un*-clothed," he says, but "clothed *upon*, that what is mortal may be swallowed up by life." In him, his human nature, his human affections, his human gifts, were possessed and glorified by a new and heavenly life; they remained; he speaks of them in the text, and in his humility he calls them his infirmity. He was not stripped of nature, but clothed with grace and the power of Christ, and therefore he *glories* in his infirmity. This is the subject on which I wish to enlarge.

A heathen poet[5] has said, Homo sum, humani nihil a me alienum puto. "I am a man; nothing human is without interest to me:" and the sentiment has been widely and deservedly praised. Now this, in a fullness of meaning which a heathen could not understand, is, I conceive, the characteristic of this great Apostle. He is ever speaking, to use his own words, "human things," and "as a man," and "according to man," and "foolishly"; that is, human nature, the common nature of the whole race of Adam, spoke in him, acted in him, with an energetical presence, with a sort of bodily fullness, always under the sovereign command of Divine grace, but losing none of its real freedom and power because of its subordination. And the consequence is, that, having the nature of man so strong within him, he is able to enter into human nature, and to sympathize with it, with a gift peculiarly his own.

Now the most startling instance of this is this, —that, though his life prior to his conversion seems to have been so conscientious and so pure, nevertheless he does not hesitate to associate himself with the outcast heathen, and to speak as if he were one of them. St. Philip Neri[6], before he communicated, used to say, "Lord, I protest before Thee that I am good for nothing but to do evil." At confession he used to say, "I have never done one good action." He often said, "I am past hope." To a penitent he said, "Be sure of this, I am a man like my neighbors, and nothing more." Well, I mean, that somewhat in this way, St. Paul felt all his neighbors, all the whole race of Adam, to be existing in himself. He knew himself to be possessed of a nature, he was conscious of possessing a nature, which was capable of running into all the multiplicity of emotions, of devices, of purposes, and of sins, into which it had actually run in the wide world and in the multitude of men; and in that sense he bore the sins of all men, and associated himself with them, and spoke of them and himself as one. He, I say, a strict Pharisee (as he describes himself), blameless according to legal justice, conversing with all good conscience before God, serving God from his forefathers with a pure conscience, he nevertheless elsewhere speaks of himself as a profligate heathen outcast before the grace of God called him. He not only counts himself, as his birth made him, in the number of "children of wrath," but he classes himself with the heathen as "conversing in the desires of the flesh," "and fulfilling the will of the flesh." And in another Epistle, he speaks of himself, at the time he writes, as if "carnal, sold under sin"; he speaks of "sin dwelling in him," and of his "serving with the flesh the law of sin"; this, I say, when he was an Apostle confirmed in grace. And in like manner he speaks of concupiscence as if it were sin; all because he vividly apprehended, in that nature of his which grace had sanctified, what it was in its tendencies and results when deprived of grace.

And thus I account for St. Paul's liking for heathen writers, or what we now call the classics, which is very remarkable. He, the Apostle of the Gentiles, was learned in Greek letters, as Moses, the lawgiver of the Jews, his counterpart, was learned in the wisdom of the Egyptians; and he did not give up that learning when he had "learned Christ." I do not think I am exaggerating in saying so, since he goes out of his way three times to quote passages from them; once, speaking to the heathen Athenians; another time, to his converts at Corinth; and a third time, in a private Apostolic exhortation to his disciple St. Titus. And it is the more remarkable, that one of the writers whom he quotes seems to be a writer of comedies, which had no claim to be read for any high morality which they contain. Now how shall we account for this? Did St. Paul delight in what was licentious? God forbid; but he had the feeling of a guardian-angel who sees every sin of the rebellious being committed to him, who gazes at him and weeps. With this difference, that he had a sympathy with sinners, which an Angel (be it reverently said) cannot have. He was a true lover of souls. He loved poor human nature with a passionate love, and the literature of the Greeks was only its expression; and he hung over it tenderly and mournfully, wishing for its regeneration and salvation.

This is how I account for his familiar knowledge of the heathen poets. Some of the ancient Fathers consider that the Greeks were under a special dispensation of Providence, preparatory to the Gospel, though not directly from heaven as the Jewish was. Now St. Paul seems, if I may say it, to partake of this feeling; distinctly as he teaches that the heathen are in darkness, and in sin, and under the power of the Evil One, he will not allow that they are beyond the eye of Divine Mercy. On the contrary, he speaks of God as "determining their times and the limits of their habitation," that is, going along with the revolutions of history and the migrations of races, "in order that they should seek Him, if haply they may feel after Him and find Him," since, he continues, "He is not far from every one of us." Again, when the Lycaonians[7] would have worshiped him, he at once places himself on their level and reckons himself among them, and at the same time speaks of God's love of them, heathens though they were. "Ye men," he cries, "why do ye these things? We also are mortals, men like unto you;" and he adds that God in times past, though suffering all nations to walk in their own ways, "nevertheless left not Himself without testimony, doing good from heaven, giving rains and fruitful seasons, filling our hearts with food and gladness." You see, he says, "*our* hearts," not "your," as if he were one of those Gentiles; and he dwells in a kindly human way over the food, and the gladness which food causes, which the poor heathen were granted. Hence it is that he is the Apostle who especially insists on our all coming from one father, Adam; for he had pleasure in thinking that all men were brethren. "God hath made," he says, "all mankind of one"; "as in Adam all die, so in Christ all shall be made alive." I will cite but one more passage from the great Apostle on the same subject, one in which he tenderly contemplates the captivity, and the anguish, and the longing, and the deliverance of poor human nature. "The expectation of the creature," he says, that is, of human nature, "waiteth for the manifestation of the sons of God. For the creature was made subject to vanity, not willingly, but by reason of Him that made it subject, in hope; because it shall be delivered from the servitude of corruption into the liberty of the glory of the children of God. For we know that every creature groaneth and travaileth in pain until now."

These are specimens of the tender affection which the great heart of the Apostle had for all his kind, the sons of Adam: but if he felt so much for all races spread over the earth, what did he feel for his own nation! O what a special mixture, bitter and sweet, of generous pride (if I may so speak), but of piercing, overwhelming anguish, did the thought of the race of Israel inflict upon him! the highest of nations and the lowest, his own dear people, whose glories were before his imagination and in his affection from his childhood, who had the birthright and the promise, yet who, instead of making use of them, had madly thrown them away! Alas, alas, and he himself had once been a partner in their madness, and was only saved from his infatuation by the miraculous power of God! O dearest ones, O glorious race, O miserably fallen! so great and so abject! This is his tone in speaking of the Jews, at once a Jeremias and a David; David in his patriotic care for them, and Jeremias in his plaintive and resigned denunciations.

Consider his words: "I speak the truth in Christ," he says; "I lie not, my conscience bearing me witness in the Holy Ghost; that I have great sadness and continual sorrow in my heart." In spite of visions and ecstasies, in spite of his wonderful election, in spite of his manifold gifts, in spite of the cares of his Apostolate and "the solicitude for all the churches"—you would think he had had enough otherwise both to grieve him and to gladden him—but no, this special contemplation remains ever before his mind and in his heart. I mean, the state of his own poor people, who were in mad enmity against the promised Saviour, who had for centuries after centuries looked forward for the Hope of Israel, prepared the way for it, heralded it, suffered for it, cherished and protected it, yet, when it came, rejected it, and lost the fruit of their long patience. "Who are Israelites," he says, mournfully lingering over their past glories, "who are Israelites, to whom belongeth the adoption of children, and the glory, and the testament, and the giving of wealth, and the service of God, and the promises: whose are the fathers, and of whom is Christ according to the flesh, who is over all things, God blessed forever. Amen."

What a hard thing it was for him to give them up! He pleaded for them, while they were persecuting his Lord and himself. He reminded his Lord that he himself had also been that Lord's persecutor, and why not try them a little longer? "Lord," he said, "they know that I cast into prison, and beat in every synagogue, them that believed in Thee. And, when the blood of Stephen[8], Thy witness, was shed, I stood by and consented, and kept the garments of them that killed him." You see, his old frame of mind, the feelings and notions under which he persecuted his Lord, were ever distinctly before him, and he realized them as if they were still his own. "I bear them witness," he says, "that they have a zeal of God, but not according to knowledge." O blind! blind! he seems to say; O that there should be so much of good in them, so much zeal, so much of religious purpose, so much of steadfastness, such resolve like Josias[9], Mathathias[10], or Machabæus[11], to keep the whole law, and honor Moses and the Prophets, but all spoiled, all undone, by one fatal sin! And what is he prompted to do? Moses, on one occasion, desired to suffer instead of his rebellious people: "Either forgive them this trespass," he said, "or if Thou do not, strike me out of the book." And now, when the New Law was in course of promulgation, and the chosen race was committing the same sin, its great Apostle desired the same: "I wished myself," he says, speaking of the agony he had passed through, "I wished myself to be an anathema from Christ, for my brethren, who are my kinsmen according to the flesh." And then, when all was in vain, when they remained obdurate, and the high decree of God took effect, still he would not, out of very affection for them, he would not allow after all that they were reprobate. He comforted himself with the thought of how many were the exceptions to so dismal a sentence. "Hath God cast away His people?" he asks; "God forbid. For I also am an Israelite, of the seed of Abraham, of the tribe of Benjamin." "All are not Israelites that are of Israel." And he dwells upon his confident anticipation of their recovery in time to come. "They are enemies," he says, writing to the Romans, "for your sakes;" that is, you have gained by their loss; "but they are most dear for the sake of the fathers; for the gifts and the calling of God are without repentance." "Blindness in part has happened to Israel, until the fullness of the Gentiles should come in; and so all Israel should be saved."

My Brethren, I have now explained to a certain extent what I meant when I spoke of St. Paul's characteristic gift, as being a special apprehension of human nature as a fact, and an intimate familiarity with it as an object of continual contemplation and affection. He made it his own to the very full, instead of annihilating it; he sympathized with it, while he mortified it by penance, while he sanctified it by the grace given him. Though he had never been a heathen, though he was no longer a Jew, yet he was a heathen in capability, as I may say, and a Jew in the history of the past. His vivid imagination enabled him to throw himself into the state of heathenism, with all those tendencies which lay dormant in his human nature carried out, and its infirmities developed into sin. His wakeful memory enabled him to recall those past feelings and ideas of a Jew, which in the case of others a miraculous conversion might have obliterated; and thus, while he was a Saint inferior to none, he was emphatically still a man, and to his own apprehension still a sinner. And this being so, do you not see, my brethren, how well fitted he was for the office of an Ecumenical Doctor[12], and an Apostle, not of the Jews only, but of the Gentiles? The Almighty sometimes works by miracle, but commonly He prepares His instruments by methods of this world; and, as He draws souls to Him, "by the cords of Adam," so does He select them for His use according to their natural powers. St. John, who lay upon His breast, whose book was the sacred heart of Jesus, and whose special philosophy was the "scientia sanctorum," *he* was not chosen to be the Doctor of the Nations. St. Peter, taught in the mysteries of the Creed, the Arbiter of doctrine and the Ruler of the faithful, he too was passed over in this work. To him specially was it given to preach to the world, who knew the world; he subdued the heart, who understood the heart. It was his sympathy that was his means of influence; it was his affectionateness which was his title and instrument of empire. "I became to the Jews a Jew," he says, "that I might gain the Jews; to them that are under the Law, as if I were under the Law, that I might gain them that were under the Law. To those that were without the Law, as if I were without the Law, that I might gain them that were without the Law. To the weak I became weak, that I might gain the weak. I became all things to all men, that I might save all."

And now, my brethren, my time is out[13], before I have well begun my subject. For how can I be said yet to have entered upon the great Apostle, when I have not yet touched upon his Christian affections, and his bearing towards the children of God? As yet I have chiefly spoken of his sympathy with human nature unassisted and unregenerate; not of that yearning of his heart, as it showed itself in action under the grace of the Redeemer. But perhaps it is most suitable on the feast of his Conversion, to stop at that point at which the day leaves him; and perhaps too it will be permitted to me on a future occasion to attempt, if it be not presumption, to speak of him again.

Meanwhile, may this glorious Apostle, this sweetest of inspired writers, this most touching and winning of teachers, may he do me some good turn, who have ever felt a special devotion towards him! May this great Saint, this man of large mind, of various sympathies, of affectionate heart, have a kind thought for every one of us here according to our respective needs! He has carried his human thoughts and feelings with him to his throne above; and, though he sees the Infinite and Eternal Essence, he still remembers well that troublous, restless ocean below, of hopes and fears, of impulses and aspirations, of efforts and failures, which is now what it was when he was here. Let us beg him to intercede for us with the Majesty on high, that we too may have some portion of that tenderness, compassion, mutual affection, love of brotherhood, abhorrence of strife and division, in which he excelled. Let us beg him especially, as we are bound, to bless the most reverend Prelate[14], under whose jurisdiction we here live, and whose feast day this is; that the great name of Paul may be to him a tower of strength and fount of consolation now, and in death, and in the day of account.

---

1. **Introductory Note.** This discourse on St. Paul, delivered in Dublin, 1857, forms one of the *Sermons on Various Occasions*. Paul—that godlike man who longed to be anathema from Christ if thereby he could serve the brethren—was Newman's saint by predilection; and allusions to his character and mission are frequent in the Cardinal's writings. As these selections for study began with Saul, they may well finish with a sketch of the greater Saul—the Apostle of the Gentiles.
2. Faith, hope, and charity; so-called because God is their direct object and motive.
3. The Holy Eucharist. "I am the living bread which came down from heaven." St. John vi. 51. "And the bread that I will give is my flesh for the life of the world." St. John vi. 52.
4. Commemorated January 25.
5. Terence. There is much philanthropy in these latter times,—even to altruism,—but less of charity, which loves the neighbor for God's sake.
6. Lived in the sixteenth century. Founder of the Oratorians, a congregation devoted to preaching and works of charity. Newman introduced the Oratorians into England.
7. People of south central part of Asia Minor; evangelized by St. Paul.
8. The first Christian martyr; stoned to death by the Jews, outside the walls of Jerusalem.
9. King of Juda, seventh century B.C. A great warrior and defender of the Jewish religion.
10. "Gift of God." Lived in the second century B.C. and fought bravely in defense of Juda during the bloody persecutions of Antiochus. He appointed Judas Machabeus, the most famous of his five sons, to succeed him in the struggle.
11. "The Hammer." Judas gained glorious victories over the Idumeans, Ammonites, and other heathen tribes, and the Bible immortalizes his character as that of one of the greatest of the sons of Juda. "He made Jacob glad with his works and his memory is blessed forever." The books of the Machabees are the history of the final struggles of the Jews against their Syrian and Persian foes.
12. A teacher of the universal Church.
13. This conclusion exhibits once more the felicity of diction, the delicate rhythm of structure, the simple grace, the direct force—above all, the unconsciousness, almost

disdain of producing literary effect, that everywhere characterize Newman's writings, whatever be the subject.

14. Paul Cardinal Cullen, primate of Ireland in 1850. Transcriber's Note. There were a few minor printers' errors which have been amended. For example, ascendency is now ascendancy, rebrobate is now reprobate and offically is now officially.In the original book the line numbers ran from 1 to 30 on each page. In the Notes, the first figure represents the page number and the second number represents the line number. For example, in the note: **Manna.** Miraculous food supplied to the Jews, wandering in the desert of Sin, after their exodus from Egypt. The taste of manna was that of flour mixed with honey. the 13 refers to the page number and the 7 refers to the line number on that page.Links to the end notes have been made to the nearest line number, for the convenience of the reader.